Not Rocket Science

A Story of No Kill Animal Shelter Advocacy in Huntsville, Alabama

Aubrie Kavanaugh

Portions of this book which refer to the No Kill Equation are reprinted with permission of Nathan Winograd and the No Kill Advocacy Center, Inc.

Portions of blogs written by Mike Fry, Christie Keith and Shirley Marsh are used with permission. Quote from Mitch Schneider used with permission.

Cover design using public image from NASA; Photo Identifier GPN-2002-000130.

Printed in the United States of America

First Printing, 2019
Second Printing, 2021

ISBN 9781792840364

For my parents, Janet and Bill, who taught me about unconditional love, compassion, tolerance, and the value of all living creatures. I wish you could have stayed.

We stood at the gates of hell and shot
the fire with water guns.
Through the storms got our umbrellas
and drew the sun inside each one.
We saw the sun.

— Fisher, "Water Guns"

Table of Contents

Not Rocket Science

Changes

No Good Time to Say Farewell

On April 22, 2006, we decided to have our 16-year old German Shepherd/coyote mix dog, Snake, euthanized. My husband, Rich, had rescued her in 1992 with the help of the Lassen County Game Warden in Northern California. She spent the first two years of her life chained to a tree with a heavy logging chain, and the only way to save her was an adopter who was experienced with dog behavior and trauma.

It took time to take her from a dog who "pancaked"[1] and did not trust people to a dog who was confident and loyal. Snake was a sight to behold. She looked like a German Shepherd in the body of a coyote, all muscle and heart. She was incredibly smart and a true athlete. She lived to chase a Frisbee, jumping and twisting in the air to catch her toy. She was very protective of us, and we were always careful with her around other dogs and other people; she was part domestic dog and part wild child.

Snake had been declining for years, and we knew the day would come when we would have to make the decision that was worst for us, but best for her. She had become trapped in a body that no longer functioned well. She had trouble digesting food, was intermittently incontinent and had mobility issues. When she began to have cognitive issues in addition to her physical issues, we knew it was time. On a sunny Saturday morning,

---

[1]"Pancaking" refers to a submissive behavior when a dog is nervous. He lowers his or her belly to the ground and creeps forward on his elbows and haunches.

Rich called our veterinarian and asked her to come to the house; this was something we had arranged months in advance.

I took her for one last walk as I tried to hide my anguish. I worried she would feed off my emotions and be scared. It was a beautiful day, and she seemed to be feeling pretty good, but we knew it was time if we were to save her from suffering and pain. We didn't realize until later that it was Earth Day. We buried her on our rural property in a breathtaking casket Rich had been quietly building for months.

Even when we know ahead of time that the ones we love are going to leave us, dealing with that loss is another matter entirely. The void left by the absence of someone you have lived with for so long is both striking and shocking.

We told ourselves Snake had a long and wonderful life because those things were true. Having her euthanized was one of the hardest things we had ever done, and so we struggled with the decision. Did we let her go too soon? Had we waited for too long? The decision was agonizing even though it was right.

In the weeks and months after Snake left us, I didn't cope particularly well. I felt broken. I knew in my mind that we had done the right thing for her, but emotionally, I just was not able to come to terms with the loss.

After about a month of struggling through most days, I decided to start donating in Snake's honor to the animal shelter in the city where I work, to help myself feel better. The thought was that by helping other animals, I could honor the years shared with our beloved girl. My donations weren't much; just a few items I presumed the shelter didn't budget for and could use: dog biscuits, dryer sheets, fleece blankets, dog toys. I drove to the shelter on the 22nd of each month, dropped off my box of items and drove away, feeling that maybe I had helped other dogs have a better day.

Shock and Awe

It was late July 2006, and I had already dropped off my donation box for the month. I was on the website for the animal shelter looking for a donation wish list when I ran across a video promoting the shelter. I decided to watch it, thinking that if it was good, I would share it with others to encourage them to adopt an animal from the shelter.

It was rather mundane as shelter videos go and seemed to run longer than I thought some people might tolerate. The first ten minutes or so were positive, showing the inside of the shelter, some of the animals and some of the employees.

Then it changed remarkably. It became dark and somewhat menacing, from what I recall. It may not really have been that way, but memory is what it is. It got to a point where a dog was being taken from a kennel and walked down a hallway as the shelter director's voice explained that they did their best, but they just could not save them all. The dog was a Beagle. Tail wagging, happy to be alive and oblivious to what I now feared was coming. It took a matter of seconds for me to realize what was going on. The dog was being taken to the "E room" to be destroyed. The video didn't show the act of taking his life, that I know of, but I fumbled as I scrambled to find my computer mouse; I could not stop the video fast enough. My heart began to pound in my ears. I started breathing faster, and I gasped before the tears began to form in my eyes.

I was shocked. I was outraged.

Five Words

I emailed the shelter the next day, after I had calmed down. I wrote that I thought it was inappropriate to have the video on a website that could be accessed by children. I asked if the dog in the video was destroyed or if he had just been filmed for the purposes of the video.

Words have incredible power over us. Taken individually, they are ordinarily harmless. Put into sentences, they still may not affect us greatly absent context.

The reply to my email was short and direct. It confirmed that the dog in the video had been destroyed. It said:

"Nobody wants Beagles these days."

For all the emotion behind the words, it could just as easily have said, "old couches get destroyed" or "broken tables go to the dump" or "paper plates go in the trash." The dismissive tone used to refer to the death of this dog offended me and angered me. He was healthy. He was happy. He could have been someone's lost dog or could have become someone's beloved companion.

In the wake of making a conscious decision to have our geriatric dog euthanized, the fact that a perfectly healthy dog was destroyed with so little regard for his life was appalling to me. I know exactly what euthanasia means, as does any person who has made the choice to end the life of a beloved pet to prevent or alleviate suffering. What happened to the Beagle I saw in the video was not euthanasia. It was killing. And I knew in my heart that it was both wrong and unnecessary.

The day I watched the video and learned what was happening at my local animal shelter was an epiphany for me. My tipping point. I got upset, and then I got angry, and then I got smart, and learned that this was happening not only at my local animal shelter, but also across the country. Millions of perfectly healthy and treatable animals were being killed in "shelters" every year for no good reason at all. And I wanted it to stop.

So, I became a no kill advocate.

My story became part of the bigger story of animal welfare awareness and advocacy in Huntsville, Alabama. This is not my story alone; it is the story of a group of advocates who banded together to promote a culture in the community related to shelter animals.

I have omitted the names of public officials involved in this story not to protect their identities, but because their names are not significant to understanding the path we took. Our story is about a process and has never been about individual people.

Not Rocket Science

Understanding Some Basics About Animal Shelters and No Kill Philosophies

American Values, American Behavior

At the time I had my unwelcome epiphany about what was happening at my local animal shelter, I was like most Americans who love animals. I had grown up in a household where animals were family members to be loved and respected—quirks and all. They were not humans, but they were shown the same respect and compassion shown to humans. For the first forty-plus years of my life, I considered myself animal aware just because I loved animals.

But was it enough to love animals in a general sense? I found out later that it was not; I was essentially clueless when it came to important issues related to the companion animals with whom we share our homes, our hearts and our lives.

I was not alone in my ignorance. I think it is human nature to focus on what is on our personal radar. We may have some general awareness of issues that don't affect us personally, but they occupy the fringes of our focus, and we really don't spend much time thinking about them. We focus instead on what is important to us each and every day: our families, our faith, our jobs, our friends, our own animals.

America is an animal-friendly society. According to the 2017-2018 National Pet Owners Survey conducted by the American Pet Products Association (APPA), approximately sixty-eight percent of U.S. households own a pet—about 85 million families Most of us consider our companion animals family members. We recognize that they enrich our lives in countless ways, improve our physical and mental health, and make us better people. We value the fact that they don't care what we look like, where we live, what we do for a living or how much money we make; their love for us is unconditional. And we agonize over our decisions when the time comes to say farewell to them due to advanced age or disease.

Most of us think it should be illegal for shelters to destroy animals unless they are suffering or are genuinely dangerous. We trust that shelters funded by our tax dollars and donations will give homeless animals that second chance. We often hold our values regarding companion animals above the values of many other cultures where animals we keep as pets are either consumed or are raised specifically to harvest their fur.

There are people in our society who should never have companion animals because they neglect them or treat them as disposable. I believe those people are in the minority. There are also people in our society, from backyard breeders to dog fighters, who engage in behavior most of us consider unethical or illegal regarding animals. Those people are also in the minority and do not represent our animal-loving society as a whole.

I have long believed that most people who share their lives with animals mean well, even if they do not always make the best choices that affect us all. There are people who allow dogs to run at large, putting the dogs and the public at risk. There are people who do not spay or neuter their animals for a host of reasons, leading to increased pet populations in our communities. There are people who fail to take steps to ensure their pets can be identified if they are displaced from home, and there are people who would tell you that they love their pets, but who have made no plans for the care of those pets in the event of the death or serious illness of the owners. When it comes to these types of people, my experience is that education goes a long way. Once we explain to people how their personal behavior and choices affect not just the community, but the way the tax-funded animal shelter operates, most people can be persuaded to make better personal choices.

I have also long believed that once "the public" is made aware of what is taking place in animal shelters using their money (and while they are, for the most part, blamed for the killing), things will change. I had to ask myself the question: If I thought I was "animal aware," but had no clue what was happening at my local animal shelter, didn't it stand to reason that most people were in the dark, just like me?

The answer was yes and no. But I had to educate myself on some basics to understand what was happening in my community and in communities like mine across the country.

After reading those five words, "nobody wants Beagles these days," I embarked on an exhaustive search to learn why healthy and treatable animals were being destroyed in shelters. Surely there was some other way for shelters to function and surely the public could be involved in that process to help bring about change. I just had to find it.

American Animal Shelters and Advocacy

Americans have been housing animals in places we call shelters for over 100 years and have been destroying healthy and treatable animals for as long as anyone can remember. Although the number of animals destroyed in our nation's shelters has declined greatly in the past 40 years, we still kill healthy and treatable animals by the millions. The No Kill Advocacy Center, Inc. estimates that approximately 2 million animals die in shelters each year (roughly 22% of dogs and 45% of cats).

Types of Animal Shelters

There are two types of animal shelters in the United States.

Municipal animal shelters are funded by tax dollars. Most are operated by cities and counties, some as joint municipal operations, and they are staffed by municipal employees. Some municipal animal shelters are operated by nonprofit organizations that hold a contract with a municipality (or municipalities); the operation is essentially outsourced to the nonprofit, but the operation is still funded by tax dollars. Most municipal animal shelters are kill shelters (see below), although that culture is changing as the American public increasingly demands better use of tax dollars in ways that are consistent with our values.

Although we call them shelters, many municipal animal facilities exist primarily for public safety purposes from an earlier era: to impound animals found running at large and to quarantine animals who have bitten someone for a state-mandated rabies hold period. Some are little more than disposal facilities in which most of the animals are killed. Absent local legislation to the contrary, these shelters are not obligated to take owned animals that are, at this stage in our history, considered property under the law. Most animal shelters do take owned animals as a form of public service even though they are not required to do so.

Nonprofit animal shelters are privately managed facilities funded by donations and grants. Many have no paid employees and are staffed and operated by volunteers. Most nonprofit animal shelters are limited admission (see below) no kill shelters. They take animals from local municipal animal shelters to reduce shelter populations and may take animals directly from the pubic to prevent those animals from entering the local municipal animal shelter.

Animal Shelter Operations

There are essentially three types of animal shelter operations in the United States.

Kill shelters. [2] In a traditional or kill shelter, animals who are suffering or irremediably ill are euthanized; dogs who present a *genuine* public safety risk are destroyed; and healthy and treatable animals are destroyed for space or convenience. The people who destroy the animals are certified to do so but are not always licensed veterinarians. A variety of methods are used to euthanize and kill animals, the most common being described as "injectable agents" (although some shelters still use gas chambers which kill animals using carbon monoxide or carbon dioxide).

Some people object to the description of shelters as kill facilities, but that description serves a purpose in our culture, in which people are becoming increasingly aware of how their tax dollars are being spent related to animals. Euthanasia (as it relates to animals) is defined as the act or practice of killing or permitting the death of a hopelessly sick or injured animal in a relatively painless way for reasons of mercy. Destroying healthy and treatable animals is not euthanasia.

---

[2]Use of the phrase "kill shelter" is somewhat controversial in animal welfare advocacy circles. Some people believe we should refer to animal shelters where healthy and treatable pets are destroyed for space or convenience as "traditional" animal shelters. Although use of the word traditional is accurate, I use the word "kill" on purpose. Ending the lives of healthy and treatable pets is not euthanasia. It is killing them. If we ever hope to end the killing of animals in places we call shelters, it is important to describe what is happening accurately, regardless of the motivations for those actions or the good intentions of the people ending the lives of the animals.

Limited admission no kill shelters. A limited admission no kill shelter is a shelter where animals are not destroyed unless they are suffering, irremediably ill or a genuine public safety risk. [3] As the name implies, these shelters limit admission by strictly controlling their intake. When the shelter is full, it does not admit any more animals until space is open. Limited admission shelters are nonprofit shelters that rely on donations to function and that receive no public support; to take in more animals than can be properly housed and cared for would quickly overwhelm the shelter operation and would be irresponsible.

Open admission/managed admission no kill shelters. These facilities operate using the same principles as limited admission facilities, but they manage intake by using progressive programs and, in some cases, a waiting list for owners to surrender animals to ensure that the shelter does not become overpopulated. These shelters only euthanize animals who are suffering, irremediably ill or a genuine public safety risk. They do not kill healthy and treatable animals for space or convenience.

---

[3]Although numerous dogs are destroyed in our nation's animal shelters for behavioral issues which are categorized in a number of ways (fear, aggression, public safety and "high arousal") experts have opined that shelter evaluations of dogs are no better than a coin toss and the number of dogs who are genuinely dangerous make up less than 1 percent of all shelter intake. Shelters are nothing at all like the homes or lives dogs may have known outside the shelter environment; it should come as no surprise to us when dogs housed in shelters do not behave in what we would consider a "normal" manner and that many show signs of fear, anxiety and stress.

It has been argued that a shelter with managed admission is not actually an open admission shelter. That is simply not true. As Christie Keith wrote in her Dogged Blog in November 2013:

> A shelter or animal control agency that responsibly manages its intake flow is still an open admission shelter. Shelters that fulfill the legal or contractual requirements of their municipality as to what animals they are required to admit, and that additionally have provisions for emergency intake for animals in immediate need, *are* open admission shelters.
>
> That doesn't change if they work with pet owners to delay intake until the shelter has room, the animal has had vaccinations, or a foster home opens up. Nor does it change if they instead work with the pet owner to try to help them keep the pet, or to find a home for the pet themselves.
>
> Managed open admission works. Unmanaged open admission is irresponsible and inhumane. They are *both* open admission.

Why Advocates Focus on Municipal Animal Shelters

Shelters are operated by municipalities and nonprofit groups. Advocates focus on municipal animal shelters for three essential reasons: money, actions and accountability.

Money. Municipal animal shelters are, in effect, a government department that provides public services. In that regard, a shelter is no different than the police, fire, parks and recreation, and public services departments. Citizens are paying for it. They may not see a line item entry on a bill like they see for water, garbage, and other municipal services, but all citizens pay for tax-funded animal shelters, whether they approve of the operation or not. Unlike municipal animal shelters, nonprofit animal shelters are funded by donations and grants and are not accountable to the public. While nonprofit shelters should ideally operate using the same progressive programs as tax-funded shelters, they are not subject to the same public criticism because they do not receive public funding.

Actions. Because municipal animal shelters are the places where healthy and treatable animals are destroyed using our money, they are the focus of our advocacy. Just because animals enter our tax-funded shelters does not mean they have to die there. Municipal shelters are required to take a variety of animals, from those found running at large to those quarantined because of a bite incident to those seized in law enforcement operations. Most are not required to take owned animals absent some local legislation. Even then, the shelter can manage that intake to control the number of animals in the shelter at any given time, and the intake need not be immediate.

Accountability. Municipal animal shelters are funded by tax dollars, making them accountable to the public being served. The public does not hesitate to complain or comment about police services, fire department response time, the timing of traffic signals, potholes in the road or garbage pickup. Because the way animal shelters handle animals involves life and death decisions, the public has an absolute right to demand the best use of their money, and to demand transparency regarding operational details and record keeping. If we do not hesitate to complain about roadway conditions, police patrol frequency or maintenance of park equipment, shouldn't we be at least equally outspoken when the lives of animals are at stake? Most people would answer that question with one word: yes.

The Chasm

Americans consider themselves animal friendly. In a national poll, 96 percent of Americans said we have a moral duty to protect animals and should have strong laws to do so. An AP-Petside Poll in 2011 revealed that three out of four Americans believe it should be illegal for shelters to kill animals if those animals are not suffering. These social attitudes are indicators of our cultural values, at least when it comes to general attitudes about animals and how our nation's animal shelters operate.

In my process of educating myself about animal welfare issues and specifically about how animal shelters in our country function, one thing became abundantly clear very early on: Even though we Americans consider ourselves animal friendly, there is a huge divide between the public being served and the shelters serving the public. I think of this divide as like a deep chasm or gorge.

On one side of the chasm is the animal-loving American public. We love our companion animals at best and value them at least. We know they are not children, but they are family members and are involved with almost every facet of our daily lives. We care for them, take them on trips, and give them toys and treats. When we lose them to time or illness, the loss can be devastating. Many of the people on "this side" of the chasm either know little about how animal shelters function or they just don't think about it unless they are personally affected by the shelter operation in some way. Most people on this side presume that shelters using our tax dollars and donations do the best they can to save animals, and that animals are only destroyed for reasons of mercy. We like to think that we are progressive and informed, and that we make good choices because we love our pets.

On the other side of the chasm are those who work in the animal sheltering industry. Some work for municipal shelters and others work at nonprofit shelters. For those on the "other side" who work at kill shelters, which routinely destroy healthy and treatable pets, life can be grim. Even if they love animals and want to help, these workers can feel overwhelmed, underpaid, misunderstood and angry — at the public. They see the people they serve or engage with as the source of the problems, often referring to the "irresponsible public" that makes mistake after mistake and that treats pets as if they are disposable. These workers feel they are forced to do acts behind closed doors that no one could possibly want to do, and yet they feel they have no choice. They think they are doing the best they can.

As an outsider looking at this situation with a fresh perspective, I thought I could see a clear solution, one that has remained clear in the many years I have been an animal welfare advocate. The fastest and easiest way for us to live our values and to ensure that the animal shelters we fund through collective resources function consistently with those values is to bridge the chasm.

The subject of animal sheltering must be put on the radar of the public so they understand what is taking place using their money, and so they can be educated to make better choices such as spaying and neutering pets, ensuring pets can be identified if lost, not allowing dogs to run at large, and making plans for pets in the event of a crisis or family emergency. And all of us need to take a long, hard look at whether we are prepared to live up to the long-term commitment that comes with being a pet caregiver and that cannot simply be abandoned when things don't go quite as we planned.

Even though many people who work in animal shelters and with rescue groups presume the public knows what is happening at local shelters and just do not care enough to make better personal decisions, that is not always true. Many, many people feel confident that all animals entering shelters are given the opportunity to be adopted, and they are mortified when we tell them that is not the case. I cannot count the number of times I have had a conversation with someone in the community where I work about the animal shelter operation and have been asked, "But, aren't all the animals made available for adoption?" When my reply has been, "No, not all of them are, and most of them are destroyed," the responses have ranged from tears to anger. Maybe people *should* know what is happening; many just do not know.

Those in the animal sheltering industry must, once and for all, take ownership and responsibility for what happens in shelters and stop presuming that every animal ends up in the shelter because of someone's irresponsibility or complacency. They must stop assuming the public knows the challenges and issues the shelter faces just because they know, acting as if the situation is obvious to all outside the shelter walls. It is not. And it makes no sense at all to say, "This is your fault, Jane Q. Public. You are to blame for the death. But won't you please volunteer and donate and foster and adopt?"

Yes, there are people who should never have pets. However, if shelters want to save more lives, they must presume the best of the public they support, be firm with the public to stop the cycle of pet surrender, and help the public understand exactly what help is needed to save the lives of healthy and treatable pets.

Pet Overpopulation vs. Shelter Overpopulation

It has long been thought that the reason millions of animals die in our nation's shelters is that we simply have too many of them. When we look at the end result, this thinking seems logical.

Not so fast.

Data from a variety of sources points to the fact that deaths in animal shelters are not due to animal overpopulation. The most compelling information suggesting that pet overpopulation is a myth is based on an evaluation of statistics. The No Kill Advocacy Center, Inc. estimates that roughly 30 million households acquire a new pet each year. To put that number into perspective, the total number of dogs and cats entering animal shelters is estimated to be around six million.

Because not all animals who enter animal shelters need new homes, the actual number of animals entering shelters who need new homes each year is estimated to be four million to five million.[4] In other words, there are about six times as many homes looking to acquire a new dog or cat than there are dogs and cats needing new homes in the United States each year.

While those figures are compelling, they are not the end of the story. The same study found that there are reasons

---

[4]Some animals need to be reunited with their families and a small percentage need to be humanely euthanized because of terminal illness or severe behavior problems.

people do not adopt animals from shelters or rescue groups. These reasons include, but are not limited to, the following:

- Shelters are often located in inconvenient places, far from where people live, work and play;
- Many shelters are open only during work hours and are not open during family-friendly hours (some people would have to take time off work or pull children out of school to reclaim or adopt an animal);
- Adoption criteria at shelters and rescue organizations are often overly restrictive and complicated; and
- Shelters are often perceived as dirty, smelly and depressing places that people do not want to visit.

For these and other reasons, people end up acquiring their pets from other sources. In other words, deaths in shelters are not so much a problem relating to the quantity of animals in the community; there is instead a problem with the marketing and availability of homeless pets. Adoption could in theory replace all population control killing right now if the public knew about the shelter animals needing homes and saw them as potential family members.

Mike Fry of No Kill Learning explained it this way in his blog post, "Call it What it Is: Not Pet Overpopulation."

> There was a time in my life when I uttered the phrase "pet overpopulation" several times a day. My family and I, after all, had spent many

years of our lives fighting to end the "pet overpopulation" crisis. The thinking was, at the time, that animal shelters in the USA killed between eight million and ten million animals annually. That was evidence enough to prove there were too many animals and not enough homes for them. We never stopped to ask ourselves if pet overpopulation existed in reality, or if the killing in animal shelters was caused by something much more insidious. Looking back on those years, that seems odd, because we had plenty of evidence that animal shelters were killing for all sorts of reasons that did not relate to any kind of "overpopulation" problem.

There was, for example, the time when my mother was trying to save a little Sheltie from one of our local humane societies. A volunteer there knew the dog was scheduled to be killed because it had mange, a very treatable ailment. The humane society would not release the dog because they had determined he was "unadoptable." The volunteer was exasperated and had called my mother for assistance. My mom, therefore, called the shelter director. He, too, told her, "No, you cannot adopt the dog. He is unadoptable." After going around and around, she eventually screamed, "He can't be unadoptable if there are people trying to adopt him!"

That shelter would go on to kill that poor dog. And, his body count would be added to the number of animals killed in animal shelters annually, which were used to maintain the belief that so-called "pet overpopulation" was real, which assumed shelters would never kill healthy or treatable animals if there were other options.

During those early years of our animal advocacy, we had many experiences with many shelters like that one: shelters choosing killing in spite of easy alternatives that were readily available to them. Therefore, looking back on it, it seems surreal that we never questioned whether "pet overpopulation" was actually real or an imaginary windmill we were fighting, Don Quixote style. But, we didn't. We went along with the cultural mind-set of the time, which said there are too many animals and not enough homes and therefore many shelters have to kill animals. We also believed that the ultimate solution was spay and neuter so that at some distant point in the future, it could result in a day when shelters didn't "have to" kill animals any more.

Since that time, other people have done the hard work of quantifying the supply and demand of companion animals, objectively proving that there are plenty of homes in the U.S. available to save every single healthy or treatable pet that enters an animal shelter. And, that has certainly been true all of my life. The real reasons shelters kill healthy and treatable pets is because they have failed to implement the programs that will save them. Too many shelters like to talk about so-called pet overpopulation, because doing so excuses the killing they are doing. It implies there is some terrible thing outside of their control that makes them respond in this fatal way. But, it is just not true.

What people think of as "pet overpopulation" is actually "shelter overpopulation," which occurs when animal shelters take in more animals than they leave alive. That happens for two primary reasons: They take in animals that do not need "rescue" (like healthy, free-roaming cats) and they make getting animals out alive too difficult. They also fail to help people keep their pets in their homes, don't do what they should to return stray animals to their families, and more. By changing those things, any animal shelter can stop killing overnight. For all of those reasons, we should stop using the phrase "pet overpopulation" and call it what it really is: shelter overpopulation.

Consider these words the next time someone tells you that animals die in shelters because we have too many of them. The issue is not one of too many animals in general; it is a problem of too many animals *in the animal shelter*.

The Burden of Change

I spent a lot of time considering the common arguments against animal shelter reform. It seemed clear to me: If there are methods we can use to save animals, why not embrace them fully? I read time and time again that the death of animals in animal shelters was not the fault of the shelter leadership, but the fault of the public. I was shocked by the number of people who seemed more than willing to forgive the deaths of animals while happily giving the people making life and death decisions a free pass. If we, as a society, are outraged by stories on the news about animal collectors, animal abuse, puppy mills or dog fighting, why are we not equally outraged by the killing of perfectly healthy and treatable animals using our money?

One of the most common arguments against animal shelter reform is that the people speaking out for a better approach cannot engage in free speech absent performing certain acts to make them worthy of that speech. Advocates have heard countless times over the years that they have to be "nicer" regarding advocacy and that if they do not volunteer in the shelters they seek to change, they really don't care. They are told that if they would just (fill in the blank), our local animal shelters would be able to save more animals. The most commonly used fill-in-the-blank option is the word "volunteer," and other words include foster, adopt, donate, and support.

There was a social media post about this very subject last year in which a shelter director openly wrote: "Shelters need REAL help and STOP with the SUGGESTIONS until you've actually physically helped in the shelter, fostered at least three pets, attended two off-site events, done adoption counseling for ten-plus adoptions and taken back pets from at least one failed adoption that you approved. Once you are a true rescue/shelter warrior and part of my tribe, I will listen." What this shelter director apparently forgot is that she is a public servant who is inherently subject to criticism. That criticism is called free speech and is the right of every citizen, not just those who meet a certain set of criteria of which the public official approves.[5]

As far as the "you should be nicer" or the "can't we all just get along" argument, the reality is that the lives of animals are at stake. Respectful communication and diplomacy are obviously preferred, but the tone we use to ask shelters to stop killing healthy and treatable animals is not relevant at all. There is no polite way to handle what we call "the ask" of municipal officials and animal-shelter leadership. It is sufficient to say, "Please stop killing animals," "these methods will help you do that right away" and "these people can help you because they have proven experience. Please call them." When a house is on fire, no one stands outside debating how to save lives and stop the blaze in ways that won't offend anyone. The focus is on the task at hand. When people tell no kill advocates they should focus on getting along

---

[5]As a U.S. Army veteran, I have strong opinions about free speech. I not only see free speech as a right of all American citizens, but I would argue that it is our responsibility to speak out on matters of public concern. If issues are important enough for us to be outraged or angry, then they must be important enough for us to speak out and express ourselves to those who govern us.

or say that the method of communication is too direct, they have put the focus on the messenger and have diverted attention away from the fact that the message is necessary in the first place.

The "if you would only volunteer" argument is also a deflection. There are people who volunteer at kill shelters and do so proudly. Many would tell you they are providing much-needed services, giving the animals scheduled to die "good endings" by taking them for a walk or giving them special treats before they are killed. The fact that some people are willing to volunteer to facilitate the process of killing healthy and treatable animals is disturbing to most advocates. These volunteers surely mean well, but the truth is that they are complicit in the process, and their silence is their consent. They are enabling the very killing that most of us find abhorrent.

The majority of people who care about animals and know that the local shelter is destroying healthy and treatable animals refuse to volunteer there and be part of a broken system that does not operate consistently with their values. Who would want to volunteer in an animal shelter and engage with healthy and treatable animals one day, only to come back the next day and find them gone not to an adoptive home, foster home or rescue group, but instead out the back door in a body bag?

If the argument is really that volunteering is the only way to save the lives of more animals, there really are other options. Plans could easily be made to get help from local jails by using inmate labor, or by having the court refer people to the shelter to fulfill community service obligations. A host of programs across the country have shown that using inmates to help care for animals helps the inmates as much as it helps the animals.

The willingness of citizens to volunteer at their tax-funded animal shelters is very important to the process of keeping animals alive, but it is not THE answer and is not a prerequisite to free speech. Once a community demonstrates that the healthy and treatable animals in the shelter are no longer at risk, people are much more apt to spend time helping the shelter. They feel confident that the animals with whom they interact will end up leaving the shelter not in trash bags but instead with adopters, fosters and rescue groups.

The burden of change is not the responsibility of advocates to carry. Everything changes when those responsible for making life and death decisions regarding shelter animals choose life, take responsibility for what happens in their buildings and then invite the public they serve to be part of a new and better future.

No Kill Basics

I learned about a lot of animal welfare subjects following my epiphany: puppy mills, breed bans, aggression in dogs, the importance of spaying and neutering. The most important subject that relates to this story and animal shelter reform is the concept of "no kill."

What No Kill Means

If you've heard the phrase "no kill" but you aren't sure what it means, you're not alone. Some people have come to equate the phrase as being very literal (meaning that no animals are ever destroyed), and they accuse people who support no kill concepts of advocating institutionalized hoarding. Nothing could be further from the truth.

No kill is a culture in which healthy and treatable animals are not destroyed in our shelters for space, convenience or following some tradition using our tax dollars or donations. In this culture, the only animals destroyed are those who are suffering, irremediably ill or so genuinely aggressive (as opposed to scared or traumatized) that they are unsafe to have in our communities (and for which no sanctuary placement is available).

No kill does not mean that no animals ever die. To keep animals alive when they are truly suffering or are so genuinely broken because of cognitive issues that they present a danger to the public would be unethical and irresponsible. Ending the lives of those animals is euthanasia because it is done for reasons of mercy and not for expediency.

No kill is a philosophy that says the lives of all companion animals have value and that those animals must be treated as individuals, worthy of our time and attention to keep them alive. In this philosophy, homeless animals are treated as having been someone's beloved companion or as being capable of being that companion. They are essentially given the benefit of the doubt, treated as adoptable and not blamed for the fact that they need our help.

No kill is not about simply keeping animals alive, regardless of the conditions in which they live. It does not allow animals' physical, psychological or emotional well-being to be compromised just so we can say "they are alive" and "we did not destroy them."

When animals are collected on rural properties out of the knowledge and view of the public and law enforcement authorities, **that is not no kill**. That is essentially hoarding, and more often than not, it also involves neglect and abuse (and sometimes mental health issues).

When animals are kept at a "sanctuary" that does not function within its financial and physical ability to properly care for and then place those animals in homes, **it is not no kill**. Overwhelmed sanctuaries are little more than animal prisons where the animals and the people caring for them are under incredible amounts of stress, often leading to disaster. It is not uncommon for us to hear stories about so-called sanctuaries that have been subject to law enforcement operations, or for which national animal welfare groups have been called upon to remove large numbers of animals because of inhumane conditions.

No kill is about values and hope and compassion, and about doing our very best for companion animals because we care about them and we want the very best for them. In the simplest terms, no kill means that you do not kill healthy and treatable animals. You do not kill them because it's easier than saving them. You do not kill them because that is what has historically been done. You do not kill them because you remain ignorant, willfully or otherwise, of programs that have been used to save shelter animals for decades.

Some organizations refuse to give grant money to any animal shelter that refers to itself as no kill because the grantors find the description divisive or offensive. It has even been suggested that the phrase "low kill" be used instead, as if that phrase would be easily understood by the public. It would not. The phrase no kill is now on the public radar, and people are smart enough to understand what it means once they are given a short explanation.

The No Kill Movement

The no kill movement is a social advocacy movement at its core. It is essentially a group of animal welfare advocates across the country who are working as individuals and as collaborative groups to seek animal shelter reform in various communities. The movement seeks not just to keep more animals alive, but also to change our very culture regarding how the public views shelter animals. The movement aims to help the public become part of something bigger than themselves by making better personal choices and by becoming personally invested in what happens at their local municipal shelters, using their money.

Many people believe that national animal welfare organizations are leading the charge for animal shelter reform. They are part of the process, but the people working hardest to effect change are the grassroots advocates. These are the people who work each and every day not only to help animals, but also to share what they know. They have learned from one another freely and without reservation. Most work full-time jobs in addition to their advocacy, which is a way of life. There are no days off. These are the people with the know-how, the smarts and the passion. They are the doers of the animal welfare movement who have learned from trial and error, research and networking, all for the sake of their belief system, which says we can and must do better for companion animals in our society.

What No Kill Community Means

A no kill community is a community in which no healthy and treatable animals are destroyed, either at the tax-funded municipal animal control/shelter facility or at nonprofit animal shelters. Each no kill community is a geographic hub or safe haven for animals within that area. These communities remain no kill communities by adopting progressive programs that keep animals alive and that provide services to just that geographic hub. Some no kill communities have achieved so much progress that they help neighboring communities by taking some animals from outside the geographic area and by helping outlying areas to improve themselves.

No Kill Myths and Truths

"No kill means no animals are ever put to sleep, and that's just wrong."

The no kill philosophy does not mean that no animals are ever destroyed. It means that animals who are truly suffering are euthanized because that's what the word euthanasia means: "the act of putting to death painlessly or allowing to die, as by withholding extreme medical measures, an animal suffering from an incurable, especially a painful, disease or condition." Also provided for in the no kill philosophy is the destruction of dogs who are so aggressive that they cannot be rehabilitated, even by experts, and thus pose a genuine danger to the public. In labeling a dog as aggressive, however, it must be remembered that very few dogs behave normally in shelter environments that can be anything but normal for a dog who is used to living in a completely different environment. Experts says the way dogs behave in shelters says much more about the shelter than it does about the dog.

"There just aren't enough good homes for the animals."

America is a nation of animal lovers, and we spend billions of dollars every year to care for our pets. We bring twenty-one million animals into our homes each year while shelters destroy approximately one and a half million animals each year. The problem is not too many animals and not enough homes. The problem, at least in part, is that we often do not market the animals effectively or use public relations effectively to help shelter animals find loving homes by educating the public that being homeless or a victim of circumstance is not the same as being "damaged." When we successfully reach out to and engage the public to convince them of the merits of adopting, we can adopt ourselves out of killing.

"Our shelter takes in too many animals to implement the No Kill Equation."

Open admission shelters across the country are located in diverse communities with their own economic and social challenges. Some of these shelters have high intakes of lost and homeless animals but are still saving as many as ninety-eight percent of all animals entering their facilities. Even in the most economically challenged parts of the country, many without large populations of residents, some high-intake shelters are adopting out thousands of animals each year. It can be done with the will and knowledge to make it happen.

"No kill is too expensive. Our community cannot afford it."

No kill is cost-effective, fiscally responsible, and can add to the economy of local communities. Saving the lives of animals in need is not only good policy, it ensures money is spent in ways which are consistent with public values. Killing animals is not free. People don't want their money used to end lives when that same money can be used to save lives. When people realize that embracing no kill philosophies is a matter not of spending more money, but of spending money in different ways, they support that change in business model and, in turn, provide more support to the shelter operation.

Although costs vary somewhat, it has been estimated by the No Kill Advocacy Center, Inc. to cost about $106 to impound, care for, and kill an animal, and then dispose of his or her body ($66 for impoundment and $40 for killing and disposal). The process is entirely revenue negative to the municipality; there is an expenditure with no income to offset that expenditure, regardless of how much money was spent to keep the animal alive. [6]

It makes more economic sense to adopt out animals, transfer animals to nonprofit shelters and rescue groups, and increase the number of stray animals reclaimed by their families, all of which are revenue positive activities that save the costs of killing and bring in fees and other revenues. The animals kept alive, after they leave the shelter, will require food, bowls and veterinary care at the very least. Some will have beds,

---

[6] I had a conversation about shelter spending with an advocate in North Carolina recently in which I used the following example. If a shelter takes in 5,000 animals in a year and destroys 3,000 animals, it may cost more than $300,000 to house and destroy those animals. It makes more economic sense to spend that same money in other ways to keep those animals alive. Examples are funding a spay/neuter program for low income families; hiring a shelter employee to focus on pet retention counseling, adoption counseling and managing a foster program; and contracting with a behaviorist to help develop and manage dog enrichment programs to keep dogs from degrading in the shelter environment.

toys, and treats. Their caregivers may take them to groomers, take them to doggy day care or enter them in local events or contests. Animal shelters may use local veterinary clinics and hospitals to have animals spayed or neutered before they are adopted into new homes. All this spending benefits businesses both inside and outside of the community.

"No kill shelters hold animals too long, spread disease and just amount to institutionalized hoarding."

Shelters managed using no kill philosophies prevent animals from entering the shelter in the first place and, if they do end up in the shelter, get them out quickly. Animals are kept in shelters for the least amount of time possible. Those kept in shelters are housed in conditions that optimize their physical and mental health to make them easier to adopt out, using facilities with standardized medical practices, disease mitigation programs, and enrichment programs which keep the animals intellectually stimulated. Examples of enrichment programs are dog walking programs, dog play groups, providing toys and treats to animals, reading programs (in which children read to dogs and cats), and outings which remove animals from the shelter for short periods of time to socialize them and make them visible in the community.

In some cases, animals stay in shelters longer than we would like because it takes longer for them to find a good home. This doesn't mean they are mistreated. Progressive animal shelters provide ongoing enrichment to animals whose length of stay is long, so those animals stay socialized to people, so the shelter staff can learn more about the animals' personalities, and so the animals can be prepared to be someone's beloved pet. In many circumstances, dogs who were neglected or mistreated prior to entering the shelter actually blossom in the shelter environment with proper enrichment and as they learn that people can be trusted.

"If we call our community a no kill community (or call our shelter a no kill shelter), people will just dump animals in our community."

Our ties to animals are emotional. When people are desperate, they often make poor choices, some of which are criminal. Once a community saves the lives of animals and people become aware of that, some people will knowingly break the law by either taking animals to that safe area and abandoning them or by surrendering an animal they own to a no kill shelter and claiming the animal was found running at large. It is no argument to say that a shelter should continue to kill healthy and treatable animals just to keep people from bringing animals in from other areas, as if the threat of death is a deterrent. When the shelter in an area is a kill shelter, people will still abandon animals, often in desperation, because they fear going to the animal shelter for help and they hope some kind-hearted person or rescue group will help their pet.

There are a variety of ways to try to offset issues with people bringing animals into a no kill community from other places. Some examples include having a Pet Help Desk manned by volunteers to help people overcome problems so they do not resort to illegal behavior, having information available on a fully developed website to which people can refer so they learn alternatives which help them rehome animals themselves or get other help to enable them to keep their pets, and determining which areas are most often used to abandon animals and working with law enforcement authorities to try to stop those actions.

The E Word

The most overused word related to American animal shelters is euthanasia. We toss it around like it is a good thing. In some cases, it is. In other cases, it is not.

The dictionary definition of euthanasia is easily understood: the act or practice of killing or permitting the death of hopelessly sick or injured individuals (such as persons or domestic animals) in a relatively painless way *for reasons of mercy*.

No one knows exactly when it was in the history of animal sheltering in America that we first began to use the word euthanasia to describe the killing of healthy and treatable animals for space or convenience in our tax-funded animal shelters.

Regardless of when this practice began, it has continued to the present day in earnest, and it does not serve us well as a society. Words and phrases have common meanings that help us all communicate. When we distort those words to excuse our behavior, condone our behavior or make ourselves feel better about a process we know on some level is wrong, we do a disservice to our values and to how we function collectively.

Enough already.

The fact that healthy and treatable animals are destroyed in our nation's shelters, along with animals who are injured or irremediably ill, and we dare call it all euthanasia should be a source of public shame for us all. We consider ours a progressive society. We talk about dogs being "man's best friend." We hold our values about companion animals above those of other cultures, as if we are somehow more evolved. We are not. And we should be ashamed of ourselves.

When we destroy perfectly savable animals in our shelters, we are doing just that. We are killing them. We are destroying them. The act has nothing at all to do with mercy and everything to do with complacency.

Our history has shown that the destruction of these animals is not necessary. The killing continues to take place using our money whether we are aware of it or not. And it just doesn't have to be that way. Killing animals is a choice. Saving lives is a choice. The growing number of communities walking away (if not running away) from the status quo and functioning in new ways more consistent with our values prove what can happen with some bravery and some introspection regarding proven programs that have saved the lives of shelter animals everywhere they have been fully implemented.

When healthy and treatable animals die in animal shelters, whether those shelters are funded by tax dollars or donations or both, the killing is not euthanasia. To compare that process with the heart-wrenching decision that loving animal caregivers and families make every day to prevent suffering is to devalue the lives of all animals in our society. If your beloved dog or cat ended up in an animal shelter through no fault of your own and was destroyed, would you call his death an act of euthanasia? No. You would not.

If a person was ending the lives of healthy and treatable animals outside of an animal shelter environment, we would not call that euthanasia. We would say the animals had been killed. There is absolutely no reason to use different words for what happens inside animal shelters as compared to outside animal shelters. The act is the same, regardless of location.

If we are ever to reform our broken animal sheltering system in America, we must speak plainly and not sugarcoat what is taking place using our tax dollars and our donations. Only then can we reach the rest of the public who do not realize what is taking place in their communities using their money and their donations. And only then will we be able to make the killing stop.

Other Animal Welfare Words

Some additional words used in animal welfare advocacy need to be examined to set the foundation moving forward. You may have specific ideas about what these words mean to you; animal shelters should use words in the same way the public uses those words, but that is not always the case.

Advocacy is a noun that describes the act of pleading for, supporting or recommending something. **Animal welfare advocacy** relates to actions taken or philosophies promoted that relate to animal welfare.

Adoptable is an adjective that means capable of being adopted, or suitable or eligible for adoption. What constitutes an adoptable animal varies greatly from animal shelter to animal shelter. In some shelters, neonatal animals, geriatric animals, animals with minor injuries, animals with skin conditions, or dogs who test positive for heartworm are not considered adoptable. In other shelters, all animals are considered adoptable even if they are very young, very old, very sick, have serious injuries, are blind or are at the end of their lives and need palliative care.

Attack is a verb that means to behave in a forceful, violent, hostile or aggressive way; to begin hostilities against; to blame or abuse violently or bitterly; or to try to destroy. It is not an attack to recommend or suggest that municipalities use tax dollars and donations in ways consistent with public values.

Criticize is a verb that means to find fault with, to judge or to discuss the merits and faults of something or someone. It is entirely possible to criticize a person or organization while still holding that person or organization in high regard, or while still having many positive views about that person or organization.

Constructive criticism is an adjective that means providing criticism to help improve, promote further development or promote further advancement. It is constructive because it is intended to creative positive results, as opposed to being destructive.

Criticizing an organization or providing **constructive criticism** about an organization is not an attack. These communication methods convey information about how operations or systems can be improved, particularly as they relate to public funds used for municipal purposes.

Healthy an adjective that means possessing or enjoying good health. It means otherwise free of serious injuries, diseases or conditions.

Kill is a verb that means to cause the death of a person, animal or other living thing. When the lives of healthy and treatable shelter pets are ended, they are killed. Having said that, it is never a good idea to call the people who end those lives killers or murderers. To do so is inflammatory and serves no real purpose in terms of seeking an end to that behavior.

Live Release Rate is a statistical calculation of the number of animals that leave an animal shelter alive.

This number is calculated as live outcomes divided by all outcomes.

Municipal accountability is the principle that governments (including municipalities) are answerable to the public and responsible for their actions, decisions, and policies. Every municipality is subject to criticism and constructive criticism from the public it serves, regarding the way it governs and the ways it uses public funds.

Shelter is a noun used to describe something that covers or affords protection. Although the word shelter is often used to describe buildings in which animals are housed, many of those places are holding facilities or disposal facilities and do not deserve to be called shelters at all. A true shelter is a haven for pets that 1) treats them as individuals whose lives have meaning; and 2) treats them as someone's beloved pet or as being capable of being someone's beloved pet.

Treatable is an adjective that means capable of being treated or responding to treatment for some illness, injury, condition or behavioral issue. What constitutes a treatable animal varies greatly from animal shelter to animal shelter. In some shelters, neonatal animals, geriatric animals with minor injuries, animals with skin conditions or dogs who test positive for heartworm are not considered treatable. In other shelters, all animals are considered treatable even if they are very young, very old, very sick, have serious injuries, are blind or are at the end of their lives and need palliative care.

Method vs. Math and Live Release Rates

There was a time in the history of the no kill movement (about a decade ago) when the ordinary byproduct of saving all healthy and treatable animals was a live release rate of 90 percent. Veterinary medicine and shelter programs have improved over time, with the percentage of animals saved in many shelters now far exceeding 90 percent. In some areas of the country, tax-funded animal shelters are saving as many as 98 percent of all animals entering shelters.

The historical reference to 90 percent has had a downside, as some organizations have focused on the number as an end goal. It is not. The whole idea is to save those animals who are, well, *savable*. The result may be that 98 percent of animals are saved in one month. The result may be that 88 percent of animals are saved in the next month in the event of some mass-intake event (such as dogs seized from a puppy mill, hoarder or dog fighter) of animals who are genuinely suffering.

No kill sheltering is not at all about math and very much about method. A shelter is a no kill facility, and a community is a no kill community, when all healthy and treatable animals make it out of the animal shelter(s) alive. When the statistics are the focus, they provide political cover for a shelter to underperform by making it permissible to kill animals once the statistical threshold is reached.

I have heard numerous times about shelters that have become so fixated on the 90 percent figure that they have engaged in fraudulent recordkeeping to make the live release rate look higher than it really is. Some shelters have gone so far as to label large groups of animals as "unadoptable" and then exclude those animals from statistical computations as they focus on the 90 percent figure to "prove" they are a no kill shelter.

Even though the focus is not on the math, there is some value in tracking statistics as a measure of progress. A shelter with a live release rate of 50 percent is essentially destroying half of the animals entrusted to its care. A shelter with a live release of 90 percent has developed programs to keep animals alive. A shelter with a live release rate of 98 percent has fine-tuned operations and is destroying only those animals who are genuinely suffering and the very small percentage of dogs who are genuinely so aggressive that they present a public safety risk.

Different organizations across the country use a variety of methods to compute shelter statistics regarding animal "intakes" and "outcomes." There is an Asilomar Accords[7] Live Release Rate, an Asilomar Accords "Lite" Live Release Rate, an ASPCA (American Society for the Prevention of Cruelty to Animals) Live Release Rate, and

---

[7]The Asilomar Accords was a meeting in 2004 attended by leaders of some national animal welfare organizations. Definitions were developed to categorize shelter animals and track them statistically (for example: healthy, unhealthy, treatable, untreatable). Because the definitions do not comport with the use of the same words by the public, some people see the Accords as a cop-out and an effort to protect the status quo at a time when the no kill movement was gaining momentum.

a Save Rate. The Humane Society of the United States provides a form to compute shelter statistics.:

> *To check the accuracy of the shelter data you've compiled, the Beginning Shelter Count (A) plus the Adjusted Total Intake (H) should equal the Total Outcomes (V) plus the Ending Shelter Count (W): A + H = V + W.*

The methods these organizations use are enough to make your head spin, which is not necessary at all. The way to compute the live release rate is simple:

live outcomes divided by total outcomes

Live outcomes are what the name implies: animals released from the facility alive. This includes the number of animals adopted, the number of animals returned to their owners, the number of animals transferred to rescue groups, and the number of cats released outside as part of community TNR (trap, neuter, return) programs.

Other outcomes are what the name implies: animals not released from the facility live. This includes the numbers of animals euthanized, lost, dead and euthanized at the request of the owner. Some calculation methods that large national animal welfare organizations use do not include ORE (owner requested euthanasia) in the calculations. When computing the live release rate, the focus is on those animals released alive; this means that all the animals no longer alive are included in the calculations. Two examples are:

Example: 1

Adoptions		100
returned to owner		50
transferred to rescue	50	
cat live release	25	
live outcomes =		225

euthanized	5
died/lost in care	2
ORE	1
other outcomes =	8

total outcomes = 225 + 8 = 233
live outcomes (225) divided by total outcomes (233) =
97 percent live release rate

Example 2:

Adoptions		75
returned to owner		15
transferred to rescue	10	
cat live release		0
live outcomes =		100

euthanized	103
died/lost in care	15
ORE	15
other outcomes =	133

total outcomes = 100 + 133 = 233
live outcomes (100) divided by total outcomes (233)
=43 percent live release rate

The Opposition to Animal Shelter Reform

I was amazed at the information I read on the internet and on social media against the idea of animal shelter reform, as if it is a bad thing. This made no sense to me at all. If your dog or cat was lost and ended up in an animal shelter, would you want the shelter to be a kill facility or a no kill facility? Would you want your pet killed because the people running the operation presumed you just did not care enough to keep your pet safe? Or would you want your pet kept alive? I know my answer.

It has been said that if we had never destroyed healthy and treatable animals in places called shelters, and that if we started doing it now, people would be outraged. The reality is that we have been destroying healthy and treatable animals in shelters for decades. Far fewer animals die in our shelters now than were destroyed years ago, as the public has become increasingly engaged in what takes place at municipal animal shelters and how their tax dollars are spent. For most of us, the fact that animals are killed is both shocking and unethical. We may not know exactly how to fix the broken sheltering system, but we want the killing to stop.

Certain values in our society are universal, regardless of where we come from, where we live, what we do to earn money and what political values we hold:

- You don't abuse or victimize children.
- You don't abuse or victimize the elderly.
- You don't drink and drive.

• You don't engage in any behavior that violates the sanctuary of another person's home.
• You don't kill healthy and treatable shelter animals.

As illogical as it may sound, there has historically been fierce opposition to shelter reform. Some of that opposition comes from unlikely sources.

The most understandable source of opposition comes from the people who manage or work in kill shelters. Although they may lament the killing of healthy and treatable pets, and they may know on some level that the public does not approve, they have become complacent about the killing. They claim it is necessary and unavoidable. Most shelter directors see criticism as a personal attack against them and are incapable of seeing it as criticism of an organization funded by tax dollars and answerable to the public. They argue that the shelter is doing the best it can with existing resources, and that advocates cannot possibly understand or appreciate the challenges they face every day. They argue that we should all just get along as we focus on the real enemy, which they see as an irresponsible, uncaring public that forces them to kill healthy and treatable animals against their will.

The unlikely source of opposition comes from people who are in the animal rescue community or who volunteer at a kill shelter and consider themselves animal advocates or animal lovers. These are people who would tell you that they feel strongly about helping animals and making good decisions for animals. Rather than consider why shelter advocacy is necessary, they expend an incredible amount of energy engaging in personal attacks defending the killing, a tactic that is both obstructionist and unproductive. Although they would tell us that they don't think healthy and treatable animals should be destroyed, they are very defensive of the fact that it happens every day.

All this strange behavior by people who consider themselves champions for animals and animal welfare can be explained as cognitive dissonance. In 1957, psychologist Leon Festinger proposed a theory of cognitive dissonance centered on how people try to reach internal consistency. His theory states that cognitive dissonance is created when we have attitudes, beliefs, and behaviors that conflict with one another. We naturally feel compelled to have our thoughts be consistent, and when they are not, the negative physical tension can be physically uncomfortable. Common examples are when a person knows that smoking is not healthy but still smokes, or when a person knows that driving a vehicle that hurts the environment is bad, but still drives that same vehicle.

Cognitive dissonance theory states that we routinely resolve the conflict in one of four ways: change one of the beliefs to alleviate the conflict; change our behavior to alleviate the conflict; add new thoughts to rationalize our behavior; or trivialize the inconsistency.

As it applies to people who defend the destruction of healthy and treatable animals in shelters, cognitive dissonance goes like this:

A belief (healthy and treatable animals should not be destroyed in shelters) is in conflict with a behavior: (I support a shelter that destroys healthy and treatable animals).

Method: Change a belief. *The shelter I support has no choice but to destroy healthy and treatable animals.*

Method: Change behavior. *I will not support the shelter because it destroys healthy and treatable animals.*

Method: Add new thoughts to rationalize. *The shelter I support destroys healthy and treatable animals because the public will not spay or neuter, there are too many breeders, the public is irresponsible, and I know that the people who work at the shelter I support are good people who don't want to destroy animals and are doing the best they can.*

Method: Trivialize the inconsistency. *This killing happens across the country and there really isn't any way to change it.*

Adding new thoughts and trivializing the inconsistency are the methods used most often to alleviate dissonance regarding kill shelters. It is easy to come up with a list of reasons to rationalize the destruction of animals who either were, or could have been, someone's beloved pet who ended up in a shelter because of circumstances beyond the person's control, and even if the person was looking for that animal. It is also easy to throw our hands up in the air and say the problem is too big to be overcome.

Shelter apologists use countless excuses in defense of the killing of healthy and treatable pets.

At the end of the day, the words are just that: excuses.

When No Kill Isn't

As the concept of no kill becomes more widely known, some organizations have begun to co-opt the phrase, using it in ways that are inconsistent with a social movement intended to save shelter animals. This misuse provides ammunition for opponents of shelter reform. They point to organizations that describe themselves as no kill and that behave unethically (sometimes engaging in criminal behavior) as examples of why the no kill movement is misguided and causes harm to animals. Some shelters have resorted to the deceptive task of promoting the fact that they are no kill when they truly are not.

No kill means you do not kill healthy and treatable animals. Period.

No kill does not mean that you label animals as unadoptable to make statistics look better than they truly are, or to hide the reality of killing for space or convenience. It is easy for a shelter to call itself no kill when it simply labels adoptable dogs as a public safety risk, or labels animals with treatable health conditions as having severe conditions requiring "humane" euthanasia.

The problem with these practices is that they are incredibly hard to expose, absent being physically present in the shelter or having access to detailed records for each animal destroyed. One example was uncovered in March 2018, when an audit by Broward County, Florida, revealed that the former shelter director doctored records to inflate the organization's apparent progress toward becoming a no kill facility. The shelter director had gone into the shelter's computer system and altered euthanasia records for dogs and cats to read "owner requested" to make the statistics look better.

As explained previously, some shelters present themselves as no kill by focusing on math and not on method. The deception comes into play when a shelter pronounces that it has a 90 percent live release rate and is, therefore, no kill. By focusing on the statistic alone, shelters are given political cover to destroy healthy and treatable animals by proclaiming that they have met a numerical standard that is really no standard at all. Provided the shelter is genuinely not destroying healthy and treatable animals, it is a no kill shelter. If a shelter destroys healthy and treatable animals after reaching a statistical goal for a month or a year, it is not a no kill facility.

There are also circumstances in which contracted animal shelter operations and rescue groups label themselves as no kill, knowing the public will respond in positive ways to that description, when they are engaged in criminal behavior. One example is a nonprofit organization that takes animals from kill shelters or from the public, solicits donations for those animals, and then abandons the animals or transfers them to research facilities. Another example is a contractor who agrees to provide animal control and sheltering services for a municipality on private property and is later found to have hundreds of animals, many of which are dead, dying, neglected or living in filth. Just such an instance occurred in Moulton, Alabama, in 2015 when a contracted shelter provider was arrested on 17 criminal charges stemming from her operation of the shelter at her home. Fifteen of those charges remained when she went to trial in February 2018; she was found guilty on six counts on February 23, 2018. She appealed her convictions; they were upheld.

The No Kill Equation[8]

---

[8]The No Kill Equation was first set forth in detail in Nathan Winograd's groundbreaking book, *Redemption: The Myth of Pet Overpopulation and the No Kill Revolution in America.* Although I have attempted to describe the Equation here using my own words, some of the explanations for the programs and services described here are taken from *Redemption* for the purposes of being thorough. All credit for this section of this book goes to Nathan Winograd.

The Game Changer

In 2007, Nathan Winograd published a book that was a game changer for animal lovers, animal advocates and the animal sheltering industry: *Redemption: The Myth of Pet Overpopulation and the No Kill Revolution in America*. Reading *Redemption* quite literally changed my life.

The book has proved a vital resource to animal welfare advocates across the country, like me, who were struggling to understand why so many animals died in shelters. It was also a wake-up call to the animal sheltering industry that it had essentially been doing animal sheltering wrong for decades, and that it was time to change. Shelters were part of a system that was mired in the past, and that had failed to keep pace with public values.

The book was controversial when it was published, although it is less so now. Just the name *Redemption* made some people uncomfortable. The shelter industry had destroyed millions of animals over decades, and the conventional wisdom about why was twofold: Because lots of animals entered shelters, there was an "irresponsible public," and because animals died in shelters, we simply had too many of them.

Neither of those adages has proved true. *Redemption* was the first time someone wrote openly that while some people are irresponsible, most people care about the welfare of animals, and we can harness the compassion in every community to save lives. *Redemption* was also the first time someone wrote openly that animals were dying in shelters not because we had too many of them, but because the sheltering industry had become calcified and complacent, and would fight with all it had to protect the status quo.

Redemption is both a history book and a how-to book. It helps us understand how we got from 150 years ago, when Henry Bergh (the founder of what we now refer to as the American Society for the Prevention of Cruelty to Animals) was able to bring about radical change in New York, to the present day, when animals are destroyed for no good reason in places called "shelters." *Redemption* was also the first time when someone dared to write that animal shelters were using words such as "adoptable," "heathy," "treatable" and "untreatable" in ways that were inconsistent with how the public uses those words.

Winograd did not invent the no kill movement. He took some programs he turbocharged at the San Francisco SPCA in California (to eliminate the killing of whole categories of animals like neonates) and other programs he implemented in Tompkins County, New York, and put them forth in equation form so that any (and every) animal shelter could stop the archaic practice of destroying healthy and treatable animals.

Redemption is compulsory reading for anyone who cares about how our society treats animals. More important, it is compulsory reading for those in the rescue community and shelter industry. To best help animals, rescuers need to understand from where all the animals who need help are coming. Rescuers must look at the bigger picture beyond X dog or Y cat. Rescuers have told me time and again that they don't have time to read a book about animal sheltering. I say that if they want to be part of the solution, they must make the time. They can also watch the documentary film based on the book, on Vimeo, for free. The film is called *Redemption: The No Kill Revolution in America.*

As far as shelters go, if they are ever going to end the outdated practice of destroying healthy and treatable pets, they must stop calling the killing euthanasia. They must embrace proven programs that can save lives. It is not enough to say that people who run and work in shelters care about animals. They must put those words into actions to prove that the life of every animal in the shelter has value.

For the purposes of sharing the path that we took in Huntsville, the most important subject covered in *Redemption* is the No Kill Equation.

The No Kill Equation

There are a variety of animal sheltering methodologies out there, put forth by a number of organizations to save the lives of shelter animals. All methods being used to save the lives of shelter pets are obviously a good thing.

Having said that, the No Kill Equation as set forth in *Redemption* is the only method that has been proven to work in every place it has been fully embraced and implemented. The genius of the equation is that it is easily understood and can be molded and shaped to fit the needs of any community, regardless of resources.

It is called an equation because it is an all-in way of thinking and functioning. If any one or more elements are overlooked or not used, the result falls short of the goal of saving the lives of all healthy and treatable animals. All elements of the No Kill Equation work in concert with one another, and many of them overlap.

Nathan Winograd was the first person in the no kill movement to present the programs necessary to save lives in equation form. He created what many people consider the blueprint for no kill success in any place in the country. And therein lies the genius of the equation; we do not need Winograd to come to each of our communities and rescue us from ourselves. We need only learn about the No Kill Equation; evaluate our existing resources, challenges and programs; connect with those who have used the equation before us (to learn from their successes and mistakes); and then mold and shape the equation to fit our communities.

The reason the equation works is because it is dual-purpose in nature. It keeps animals from entering the shelter in the first place (the "keep them out" elements) and gets those animals who do end up in the shelter out quickly (the "get them out" elements). This combination means the animal shelter is just that: a shelter. It is a safe haven, a safety net, a temporary place to house animals until they are returned to their home or are rehomed. When shelter intake is reduced and shelter output is increased, fewer animals are in the shelter at any given time, so costs are decreased.

I realize that most animal shelters in our country were designed to destroy animals and not to save them. A few short decades ago, millions upon millions of animals were destroyed in our nation's shelters. It is estimated that in the early 1980s, about 17 million animals died in shelters each year. Yes, 17 million.

That number has gone down drastically as our culture has changed and as we have become smarter and more progressive about how we house animals who are lost, found running at large, seized by law enforcement authorities or just in need of a new home. While many tax-funded animal shelters have no legal obligation to take owner-surrendered pets, many do because it has become a public expectation that shelters will be safety nets for animals, and because shelters want to be seen not as places of death, but instead as places of hope and new beginnings.

We can continue to promote spay and neuter of animals. We can continue to rescue animals by removing them from the shelter. But by implementing programs that keep so many animals from entering the shelter in the first place, and implementing programs which move them out of the shelter as fast as possible, we can save so many more animals and make better use of our time and our resources.

"Keep Them Out" Programs

The following programs of the No Kill Equation are "keep them out" programs. They prevent animals from entering the shelter in the first place.

Community Cat TNR Programs

There is a robust population of free-roaming cats in almost every community. Some are cats who are not social to people. Some are former house pets who were abandoned or are lost. Some were born outside but still have the capacity to be social to people. They live where they find resources, and you may only see them in the evenings or when most people are not around.

Most cats do not belong in municipal animal shelters at all. If you've ever taken your cat to the vet in your car and had him or her turn into something from a horror film, then you know lots of cats don't do well with travel and new environments. When cats end up in shelters, it becomes almost impossible to differentiate between a feral cat and a beloved pet who is traumatized. This presents a huge problem across the country; roughly half of the cats who enter shelters are destroyed even though the vast majority of them are healthy and treatable.

In a community cat TNR Program, free-roaming cats do not go to the shelter at all. TNR means trap, neuter, return. Cats are trapped, sterilized, vaccinated, and left-ear tipped for easy identification. Those cats social to people are put into foster care or homes. Those cats who are truly feral are returned to their habitat. Some would

70

say that feral cats should be relocated or destroyed. Because cats live in areas where they find food, water, and shelter, relocating them only attracts more cats. Destroying the cats is not only inhumane, but it often can result in loss of a service they provide: rodent control.

TNR is the only humane method of reducing populations of community cats while keeping cats from entering shelters, thereby saving tax dollars. When TNR programs are in place, municipalities don't need to do anything but endorse and advocate for the programs while no longer engaging in "catch and kill." In some no kill communities, funds that would otherwise be spent to catch and destroy these cats is applied to having them spayed or neutered, so rescue groups can use remaining funds in other ways (such as providing medical care to cats who can be rehomed or paying for basic needs while cats are in foster care).[9]

High Volume, Low Cost Spay/Neuter Programs

Having pets spayed or neutered makes perfect sense to most pet caregivers. Most of us will never even try to

---

[9]Some shelters have begun the practice of SNR: shelter-neuter-return. When cats enter the shelter, they are held for any requisite property hold period, but are then returned to the area where they were found. Shelter reclaim rates for cats are usually very low. The argument is that cats are more apt to find their way home from the area where they were found. There is a delicate balance in this type of program to make sure that the cats returned outside are not just abandoned. The idea is not appropriate for kittens, for cats who have been declawed, or for cats who are injured or have some health condition.

enter our pet into a formal breeding standards competition, so there is no reason to keep the pet intact. Altered pets can live two to three years longer than pets who are not sterilized. They are less prone to many diseases and cancers, and they are less apt to roam. If you've ever lost a beloved pet to age or disease, it is likely you would give almost anything to have just a few more days with him or her.

Most people who fail to have pets spayed or neutered don't think it is necessary, or they think they cannot afford it. For those who say it is not necessary, put your pet first. If you know your pet can live longer and be healthier, isn't that what you want? As far as the cost, it can be far less than the cost of caring for a litter of animals or the cost for a municipal shelter to destroy that litter of animals.[10]

Some communities have nonprofit clinics that do nothing but spay and neuter surgeries, charging much less than full-service veterinary clinics. Because spay and neuter is all these clinics do, the people who work there are experts at the process.

---

[10]There is some disagreement about the appropriate age to spay/neuter animals. Many shelters spay/neuter animals as young as eight weeks old so they can be adopted into new homes while ensuring that they do not add to pet populations by later having litters of pets. There is some evidence that spay/neuter at such a young age has physical and psychological consequences. In Alabama, shelters and rescue groups must spay/neuter animals prior to adoption or enter into a written agreement with the adopter to ensure the animal is sterilized within 30 days after acquisition of the animal (or within 30 days of the sexual maturity of an animal).

Other communities have taken steps to reduce pet populations by investing in spay and neuter programs, or completely covering the costs of spay and neuter surgeries, for pets of low-income or fixed-income families. This type of program is not to be confused with the concept of mandatory spay/neuter laws, which every national animal welfare organization opposes, and which leads to increased shelter intake over time regardless of any initial success.

Pet Retention Programs

Our ties with animals are emotional. When we are backed into a corner, we often don't think clearly enough, and we engage in irrational behavior. When the municipal shelter is not seen as a place of refuge or rescue, people will often knowingly break the law to avoid taking their animal to the shelter or seeking the advice of the shelter staff. The person would rather risk arrest and hope for the best.

Although municipal shelters are referred to as open admission, the designation does not mean that they should simply accept owner-surrendered animals without any questions asked. When shelters do that, they learn nothing about the history of the animals, and they lose wonderful opportunities to keep animals where they belong: in existing homes. Studies have shown that simply having animal surrender counseling leads people to keep their pets more than half the time.

Pet Retention Programs keep animals from entering the shelter by helping people overcome obstacles, whether they are short- or long-term. These programs get people to slow down, think clearly and articulate why they think they cannot keep their pet. These programs include intake counseling, pet food banks, trainer referrals, grants for veterinary care, short-term foster plans, and having a Pet Help Desk. The majority of people who have pets love them and want the best for them. It is worth the time and effort to work with caregivers to keep animals in their homes, as opposed to accepting those animals too easily, only to hold them and then destroy them.

In progressive communities, people are more apt to seek help from the animal shelter, as opposed to abandoning animals as an act of desperation. The residents of progressive communities know they will not be judged and will get the advice and help they need to keep their pet in their own home.[11]

Proactive Redemptions

Proactive redemptions is another name for return-to-owner programs that get animals back home if they escape or get lost. For municipal shelters, animal control is part of daily functioning and what the public expects. There is a balance between keeping the public safe and caring for animals. Animal control officers respond to a

---

[11]Some places that have food banks or food distribution programs for people in need also distribute pet food, particularly to homeless people. These communities see pets as having inherent value to people who are going through hard times and whose only source of support may be their pet or pets. It is better to help those people by giving them pet food than to have the animals end up in the local animal shelter.

lot of calls about dogs running at large or about free-roaming cats. When it comes to dogs and cats believed to belong to someone, the goal of proactive redemptions is to avoid taking them to the shelter and to keep them where they belong: home. The vast majority of the animals who end up in shelters and are later destroyed are actually beloved family pets. These animals should not be destroyed simply because they lack the ability to speak.

In many no kill communities, proactive redemptions boils down to actions that animal control officers take in the field. These steps include scanning animals for microchips, checking for rabies tags or identification tags, checking on a lost pet website such as Pet Harbor, and making inquiries of businesses and homes in the area. Mitch Schneider, the former Washoe County animal control director in Reno, Nevada, put it this way:

> "It starts in the field. In order to reduce the intake of these animals, something that benefits everyone, officers make every reasonable effort (check for ID, scan for a microchip, talk to area residents, etc.) to return animals to their rightful owners rather than impounding them at our facility. We are very busy in the field. However, while it might be more work initially to try to find where these animals live for the officers in the field, it is less work for staff back at the shelter. It evens out in the end. It means less animals entering the shelter and more animals going home alive. It is a win-win outcome."

Another component of this element of the No Kill Equation is ensuring that pets can be identified. This is where the public comes in, and the solutions are not complicated. Pet caregivers can ensure pets can be identified if displaced from home by having pes microchipped[12], by using collars (embroidered with a phone number) and by placing identification tags on collars (provided cat collars are breakaway collars for safety purposes). Many shelters now microchip all adopted animals so they can be easily identified if lost or misplaced from home after having been adopted.

Although many people may think microchipping isn't necessary because their pets live inside or are never unsupervised, consider how many pets are lost or displaced each year after natural disasters such as fires, floods, or tornadoes. Thousands of animals are displaced from their homes each year due to disasters and simple accidents. Microchipping can ensure that they are identified and returned to the people who love them and may be looking for them. Microchipping can also increase the odds of having your pet returned to you if he or she is stolen and ends up in the hands of law enforcement officials or at a shelter.

---

[12]A microchip is not a GPS tracking device. It is a small ampule, about the size of a grain of rice, which is implanted under the skin at animal's neck, between the shoulder blades. The chip contains a unique number, much like a bar code, that can be scanned to determine the owner to whom the chip is registered.

"Get Them Out" Programs

The following programs of the No Kill Equation are "get them out" programs that move animals out of the shelter either temporarily or permanently, and free up space.

Comprehensive Adoption Programs

When we compare the number of shelter animals needing a new home each year to the number of people in the community looking for a new pet, there are more than enough homes for these animals. Adoption is primarily an issue of marketing. People mistakenly believe that shelter animals are damaged or broken (an idea reinforced by the fact that so many are destroyed) and so they get animals from other sources. Many people don't realize that not all shelter animals get put up for adoption. Some people won't go to the shelter to adopt because they know what happens there, and they just find the whole process too depressing.

Comprehensive Adoption Programs are a huge part of getting animals out of the shelter. *Huge*. When a shelter has a "come to us" approach, is only open during hours when people are at work (and children are in school), and does not market animals in creative ways, adoptions will always fall short of what they could be.

Comprehensive programs include creative adoption promotions (pets for patriots, seniors for seniors, two-fer adoptions, five-dollar Fridays, back-in-black days, half off for halftime, home for the holidays, etc.), taking animals to the public by hosting off-site adoption events, using mobile adoption vehicles, and making adoption at the shelter easier through family-friendly hours. Shelter animals are cared for seven days a week. When a shelter is open at least six days a week, on holidays, and during hours when people can get to the shelter, it makes the adoption process immeasurably easier.

This is not a matter of the shelter being open more hours. It is about the shelter being open during hours when people can get there. It is also a matter of the shelter being perceived as an inviting place of life saving, staffed by energetic and friendly people who provide excellent customer service. People will always be more willing to adopt an animal from a location where the culture and the vibe are helpful and upbeat.

It has been said that we could be a no kill nation today if only the animals and the potential adopters were better introduced. That happens through Comprehensive Adoption Programs.

Foster Programs

Even the best shelters can be a stressful environment. Many animals are empathic. Most can see, smell, and hear things we do not. For them, a shelter is a strange and scary place, and is nothing like home. Even the most balanced of animals will not behave in a shelter the way he or she behaves outside of a shelter. This disconnect makes it difficult to identify behavioral issues and to determine which animals are social and well-adjusted.

Shelter animals in foster care are animals who are being prepared for a new life. Some are perfectly healthy. Some may have special needs. When we put animals in homes, even for short periods of time, we learn about how they behave and help them get ready to be someone's pet. Their past will never be known, but their present becomes very much known. Can he walk on a leash? Is she house-trained? Does riding in a car upset her? Does he love to play with toys? How about getting along with children or other pets? All of these questions can be answered more accurately once animals are outside of a shelter environment.

The great news is that most communities have an incredible number of resources that could become foster homes. Retirees. Soldiers. Students. There are people who may not want the long-term commitment of a pet, but who are great with pets. All of these people are excellent candidates to provide foster care.

Do you not have a pet because you think you are too old? Foster. Do you not have a pet because you want the freedom to travel a lot? You can foster. Do you want to help a deployed member of the armed forces so he does not have to surrender his beloved dog to the shelter? Fostering that dog means he can stay local and be returned to his owner when the deployment ends. Do you want to help neonatal puppies or kittens who need regular bottle feeding for a few weeks until they can eat solid food? You can foster.

Medical and Behavior Programs

Shelters need to keep animals happy and healthy, and keep animals moving efficiently through the system. To do this, shelters must put in place comprehensive vaccination, handling, cleaning, socialization, and care policies and procedures before animals get sick, and rehabilitative efforts for those who come in sick, injured, un-weaned, or traumatized.

This element of the equation starts with vaccination of all animals entering the facility to prevent the spread of illness from one pet to another. Research shows that vaccination at intake will prevent a majority of canine and feline illnesses that plague shelters. Vaccinations can be purchased in bulk and are inexpensive. Any cost for a vaccine is far less than the cost to treat sick animals or destroy and dispose of them. Maddie's Fund states, "Shelters that only vaccinate some animals, or none, or that fail to vaccinate prior to or at the instant of intake are not just increasing the risk of infectious disease outbreaks; they're guaranteeing them."

This element also includes helping animals with medical conditions or neonatal animals who require special care until they can consume solid food. A fund can be set up to offset costs for animals who need specialized care (such as treatment for heartworm or surgical procedures). Such funds are often named after a beloved pet who has died and are a way for people to help the shelter through philanthropy, perhaps to honor the memory of their own pet.

Neonatal animals can be spared by having them temporarily housed in foster homes where they are fed on an ongoing schedule and until they are old enough to consume solid food. Shelters can also help animals who are traumatized or have behavioral issues by partnering with local behaviorists, trainers, and veterinarians to evaluate these animals and make plans to find them new homes. Use of dog enrichment programs and dog play groups can go a long way toward reducing shelter stress and keeping dogs from degrading while they are in a shelter.

The medical/behavior programs element also includes analysis of the types of animals who most often end up in the shelter. By determining the source or cause of problems, those problems can be addressed.

For example, if there are ongoing issues with large numbers of puppies and kittens, those issues can be addressed (at least to a degree) with education about and promotion of spay/neuter. If there are a large number of dogs entering the shelter that were found running at large, that issue can be addressed with education and by identifying locations where dogs are commonly allowed to run at large.

Rescue Group Relationships

Many shelters have ongoing relationships with trusted rescue groups, allowing those groups to put a "rescue hold" on animals to keep them from being destroyed and then later allowing them to "pull" animals for free. Shelters that do not see local rescue groups as a life-saving resource to be respected and valued are setting themselves up for failure.

The relationship between the shelter and rescues can be refined and honed through ongoing communication about animals at risk. Rescues can be notified electronically of animals needing rescue by age, gender, suspected breed, special needs, etc. This helps rescues understand the need and do a better job of pulling animals out as quickly as possible.

While rescue groups should be given every opportunity to save animals at risk, they should not be relied upon to be "the" solution to life-saving; the shelter must do its part to place animals through comprehensive adoption programs such as pets for patriots and seniors for ·seniors while offering periodic adoption promotions to place older animals and special needs animals.

Programs That Do Both

The following programs of the No Kill Equation are dual-purpose. They reduce shelter intake and move animals through the system and out of the shelter.

Volunteer Programs

Volunteers have been described as dedicated "army of compassion" and the backbone of a no kill effort. There is never enough staff, never enough dollars to hire more staff, and always more needs than paid human resources. Volunteer programs are where people make the difference between success and failure and, for the animals, life and death.

When a shelter makes optimum use of volunteers for a variety of tasks, it can implement other elements of the No Kill Equation. Volunteers can help with TNR programs by trapping and releasing cats. They can help with pet retention programs by manning an animal help desk or helping out with owner surrender counseling. They can help at off-site adoption events. They can help facilitate a foster program. They can socialize dogs and cats by walking dogs or just spending time with the cats. They can help with neonatal puppies and kittens who need bottle feeding until they are old enough to consume solid food. The ways in which volunteers can help are limited only by the scope of our imagination.

Rescue groups and no kill shelters rely heavily on volunteers. Some people are willing to volunteer at municipal shelters that destroy savable animals, but many people will not, simply because they don't want to be complicit in the killing. The great news is that once a community announces its intention to become a no kill community, volunteers have been known to come out of the woodwork. People are much more apt to volunteer at a shelter when they do not worry that healthy and treatable animals are at risk.

Almost every community has incredible and untapped resources in terms of potential volunteers: retirees, students, soldiers, people who cannot work but are otherwise fully able to perform helpful tasks and, of course, busy people who love animals and just want to help save them and make our communities safer for them.

Public Relations/Community Involvement

Increasing adoptions, maximizing donations, recruiting volunteers and partnering with community agencies comes down to one thing: increasing a shelter's public exposure. That means consistent marketing and public relations. Public relations and marketing are the foundation of any shelter's activities and its success. To do all these things well, the shelter must be in the public eye. The way in which no kill communities develop this element of the equation is limited only by creativity.

A lot of people don't give much thought to the municipal animal shelter in their community. Some know it exists but could not tell you where it is located. Some have an idea of what takes place there and perhaps don't want to think about it. Some are active in helping the shelter and its staff, and see the wonderful things that happen there, along with the tragic. The first hurdle any shelter should overcome is making itself visible in the community; making itself relevant. When a shelter is viewed more as a place of hope and of rescue, the messaging goes a long way toward keeping animals out of the shelter and getting them out of the shelter.

Regarding the animals themselves, this element is all about marketing and making it easy to adopt shelter animals. Some people think we have a pet overpopulation problem when we really do not. There are more than enough homes for shelter animals in our communities, but people tend to get their animals from other sources because they think shelter animals must be damaged or they think all shelter animals are given the chance to be adopted. When we market animals consistently and the animals are visible in the community through off-site adoption events and use of the media, we seek the help of the public in placing animals, and we help people understand that homeless animals are just as worthy, loving, and loyal as animals from other sources.

When communities transition to no kill and people know that, incredible things can happen. Being a no kill community is a source of immense pride, and people are more apt to become part of changing the culture because they know that small acts save lives. They are proud of what can be accomplished when people work together.

Compassionate Leadership

Of all the elements of the No Kill Equation, the most important is compassionate leadership. When Nathan Winograd first put forth the equation in his book

Redemption: The Myth of Pet Overpopulation and the No Kill Revolution in America, he used the title compassionate shelter director for this element. The buck stops with the shelter director because he or she is the person who has the most influence regarding how the shelter operates. This element of the equation has since been modified to a degree by some people in our social movement, particularly as it relates to municipal shelters. It is more appropriate to describe this element as compassionate leadership.

Most shelters are run by a singular person, but all shelter directors report to others, such as boards of directors or elected officials. The person running the shelter is the key, but the way the shelter operates is decided by a group of people who make choices about tax dollars and donations.

Our Huntsville Story

Municipalities and the Huntsville Community

Every state has local governments that function below the level of state operations. These ordinarily consist of counties, cities, and towns. In some states, counties are described as parishes or boroughs. Each of these municipalities is governed by elected officials and functions using tax dollars for the greater good, making employees public servants.

Local governments are inherently subject to public criticism and comment because they exist to serve the public. Public servants are paid with tax dollars to manage local government operations, whether we approve of their behavior or not. Public service is not for everyone and we should not confuse branches of municipal government with private businesses (which are more insulated from public comment).

When it comes to subjects unrelated to animals, most of us have no issues with making our voices heard. We complain about garbage service. Potholes in the road. The timing of traffic lights. The number of police patrols in our neighborhoods. The response time of fire personnel or paramedics. For some reason, people are less apt to complain about how their local animal shelter operates, even though the lives of animals are at risk. People who are completely unaware of what happens at their local shelter obviously do not complain. Many who are aware of what is happening and who are trying to help shelter animals do not complain out of fear of being cut off from the shelter and not allowed to help animals.

Alabama is made up of towns, cities, and counties. Cities can self-legislate, meaning they can enact local laws to govern themselves, whereas counties that lack Home Rule cannot (in which case legislation must be brought through bills filed in the state legislature). The local government in Huntsville consists of a mayor and five council members. City department heads are appointed by and serve at the pleasure of the mayor. New laws are enacted by ordinances that become part of the city code.

Huntsville is situated in Madison County, Alabama, in the northern area of the state. Madison County borders the Tennessee state line. In 1811, Huntsville became the first incorporated town in Alabama. The city grew quickly from wealth generated by the cotton and railroad industries. After the Civil War, Huntsville became a center for cotton textile mills, and the population was still relatively small. That changed in early 1941, when the U.S. Army selected 35,000 acres of land adjoining the southwest area of the city to build three chemical munitions facilities that operated through World War II.

Huntsville gained national recognition during the space race of the 1960s after the U.S. government relocated a team of German rocket scientists to the area and opened a NASA center that would design the Saturn V, the rocket that sent Apollo astronauts to the moon. The Von Braun Center sits just a few miles from a full-size replica of the Saturn V rocket, which sits alongside a major west-to-east thoroughfare. The agricultural roots of the area, however, remain. You cannot drive more than two miles in the City of Huntsville or Madison County without driving past a field used to grow cotton, soybeans, or corn.

Huntsville is now the largest city in the state. Although Huntsville is best known as the home to defense and aerospace firms, other tech-related industries have also sprung up in recent decades, including many biotechnology firms. The city calls itself "The Star of Alabama," but goes by many other nicknames, including "Rocket City" and the "Heart of the Tennessee Valley." Huntsville is considered progressive not only because of the nature of its industries, but also because of its cultural diversity. Many residents who live in Huntsville and people who work in Huntsville come from other states and other countries.

Although Huntsville is considered progressive and high tech, it still faces some of the same cultural challenges as other areas of the South related to companion animals. Many people who have pets keep them exclusively outside. They are no more apt to bring a dog inside to live than they are to set a place at a dinner table for a pig. The mind-set is that animals are animals. One local elected official explained the culture of some (but certainly not all) people in the region this way: "You can say my wife is ugly and my kids are stupid, but don't tell me how to treat my dog."

The municipal animal shelter in Huntsville is operated by the City of Huntsville. It serves the geographic hub that includes the City of Huntsville and Madison County (except for the City of Madison, which manages its own animal control program). As of this writing, the shelter serves approximately 331,000 people. The City of

Not Rocket Science

Huntsville and Madison County both employ animal control personnel. The shelter director is a veterinarian who earns a six-figure salary, has a staff of 41 people and operates with an annual budget of just over $2.8 million. Although she is appointed by and serves at the pleasure of the mayor, her direct supervision is by the city administrator, who oversees multiple departments including animal services.

Having an animal shelter directed by a veterinarian may seem logical at a glance, but it's not. The job is not a veterinary job. It is an administrative job.

Animal shelter directors are responsible for managing the daily activities at an animal shelter. They supervise staff, manage animal intake and outcomes, manage a budget, handle issues with the vehicle fleet, work on policy and legislative issues, interact with elected officials and the public, and are involved with court cases. According to a study done by No Kill Learning, the core competencies for shelter directors include being action oriented, having compassion and composure, making good decisions in a timely manner, being focused on ethics and values, having integrity and the trust of the public, learning on the fly, having intellectual horsepower, having managerial courage, motivating subordinates and others, having perseverance, being politically savvy, having great problem-solving skills, focusing on results, understanding others, and being able to manage vision and purpose. When a municipality selects a veterinarian to run a department focused on animals, it has focused on functional and technical skills and ignored the core competencies that make shelter directors successful.

There is also a downside to having a veterinarian manage a shelter that I call Snow White Syndrome. People presume that because veterinarians have chosen a profession related to animal care, they surely are focused solely on the well-being of animals and would not destroy healthy and treatable animals needlessly. There is no "do no harm" oath for veterinarians, but they do take an oath to use their knowledge to protect animal health and welfare. It has been argued that veterinarians who manage shelters where healthy and treatable animals are killed (or which contract with shelters to kill healthy and treatable animals) have violated that oath.

The Wall

When I first learned what was happening at Huntsville Animal Services in 2006, I sent a letter to the mayor. I told her about the video I had found on the shelter website and about my communication with the shelter about the Beagle who had been destroyed. I told her, in essence, "We are better than this," in hopes of receiving some type of response from her.

None came.

In October 2008, I was watching the news and saw an interview of the new mayor-elect. He was a businessman who had served on the city council and won the mayoral election handily. I didn't know much about him. When I heard him speak and saw the camera pan to his dog, who was wearing a collar that read, "First Dog," I thought I might have a new ally in local government.

I sent the incoming mayor a letter on November 4, 2008, along with a copy of *Redemption*. My pitch was direct. I told him that more than 70 percent of the animals entering the shelter were being destroyed and that I thought that number was shameful in such a progressive city. I asked him for a serious evaluation of the shelter operation. I also asked him to send one person to a No Kill Conference being hosted by The Animal Law Project at George Washington University Law School and the No Kill Advocacy Center in Washington, D.C., in May 2009. I went one step further and told him I would pay the conference registration fee. The last four words in my letter were the same as what I'd told the previous mayor: "We're better than this." I didn't think much of the letter after I sent it. I did not expect a reply.

In early January 2009, I got a call from the mayor's office. The newly sworn-in mayor wanted to meet about my letter. I met with the mayor, city administrator, and shelter director on January 22, 2009. Prior to the meeting the shelter director told me the mayor had given her the copy of *Redemption* I had sent to him and that she had read it.

I didn't expect much from the meeting. I presumed I would be told about the progress which had been made at the shelter and I presumed I would be told how difficult it is for municipalities to save more animals. I spoke briefly about the No Kill Equation, and how it could be implemented in the animal shelter to save more lives. I restated my offer to send the shelter director to the No Kill Conference on my dime. My hope was that by attending the conference, the shelter director would return to Huntsville feeling empowered and having learned new ways to save the lives of animals. I felt that the No Kill Equation was easily understood and hoped she would implement the programs of the equation while networking with new contacts made at the conference. My offer was accepted; the shelter director attended the conference in May of 2009.

I sent the mayor a follow-up letter on June 4, 2009. I asked for a follow-up meeting to talk about implementing no kill programs and offered to invite leaders from the local rescue community. A few days later, I received an email from the mayor's communications director. He informed me that there was no greater champion for animals in the City of Huntsville than the shelter director. My request for a follow-up meeting was declined.

The live release rate at the animal shelter at that time was 25 percent, meaning that three out of every four animals in the building were destroyed. I had allowed myself to believe that offering help and getting a conversation started would lead city officials to act on their own to address the number of animals being destroyed.

And so it was that I hit the first of many walls.

A New Approach

Not much happened in Huntsville related to animal shelter reform from 2009 through 2011.

In 2009, I asked the shelter director to attend the 2010 No Kill Conference; she declined. I privately hoped that she was at least considering implementing the No Kill Equation on her own. I learned in 2009 that the city had invested $20,000 to implement a spay/neuter program to help low income families have pets sterilized for $5 based on where they live and their annual household income.[13] This was wonderful news and gave me hope that things were starting to change.

In the summer of 2009, I was invited to attend a meeting at a local humane society about no kill philosophies. The shelter director was there as were representatives from nonprofit organizations. I was not told in advance that I would be asked to speak; but I did my best. I was familiar enough with the No Kill Equation that I "shot from the hip" to explain the elements of the equation and why the equation was considered a one-size-fits-all solution for

---

[13]The city has continued to invest in this program, called "Fixin' Alabama" annually. It now invests almost $100,000 a year to help low income families who live in Huntsville and Madison County. This has been one factor to reduce the number of animals entering the shelter each year; the intake of animals has gone from more than 10,000 animals in 2009 to 5,100 animals in 2018.Another factor has been the work of the North Alabama Spay & Neuter Clinic, Inc. This is a high-volume/low-cost spay neuter clinic which can be used by anyone, regardless of income. It is one of only four such clinics in the state.

any community to save more lives. I felt like the information was well received by some in attendance, but was not sure if I had accomplished anything with my short presentation.

About a month later, the shelter director asked me to write a white paper advocating adoption of pit bull-type dogs. She said she needed information to use related to old guard employees and city hall, to help her adopt out more pit bull-type dogs. I knew that it would take time to write a research paper so I decided to make it general enough to be of value in any community. It was published on the Animal Law Coalition website and was used by people in other states.[14]

The Live Release Rate in 2009 was 24 percent. It was 30 percent in 2010, and it was 34 percent in 2011. Things were improving, but the progress was incredibly slow; a majority of animals entering the shelter were still destroyed.

Both my parents were diagnosed with cancer in late 2009, and we lost them within six months of each other. The subject of the animal shelter was never far from my mind, but it was only after my parents were memorialized in June 2011 that I decided the time had come to make another run at the wall.

---

[14]I revised the paper in 2014 after I saw the shelter director in a local network television series called "Leadership Perspectives" speaking about her challenges adopting out pit bull-type dogs.

Loss tends to help us focus on our priorities and what is important. I knew there was no going back for me, and I would not be able to live with myself if I did not try again to bring change to Huntsville. I had been raised in an animal-integrated household. I owed it to my parents, and to the animals with whom I have shared my life, to own my outrage and do something about what was happening in Huntsville.

As 2011 ended, I decided to try a new approach. I felt like I had been easily dismissed when I was speaking on my own. I mean, really, who was I to question how the shelter was operated? Even though I had the best of intentions and had educated myself to the point where I could speak logically on the subject, there was little motivation for city officials to listen to me at all. I presumed the city was happy with the way the shelter was operating. Why listen to a single animal advocate when you had a veterinarian running the department?

I decided to draw on concepts from my U.S. Army days. Instead of being an army of one, I decided there would be strength in numbers. I decided to present myself as one of many.

The Coalition

It has been said that politicians follow public opinion but rarely lead it. Such is the case regarding animal shelters in most communities and I felt such was the case with the shelter in Huntsville. If change was going to happen at our animal shelter more quickly, someone was going to have to speak out to demand better use of our collective resources.

In late 2011, I began reaching out to individual rescuers, nonprofit shelter directors and like-minded animal welfare advocates in the region to ask if they'd be interested in coming together to form a coalition to speak with one voice for the sake of shelter animals: No Kill Huntsville.

I purposefully did not connect with people I knew to be close with the shelter director. The function of the group would be to speak out for better, and while the focus would be municipal leadership, I knew that many people in the rescue community would personalize the message and see it as an attack on the shelter director herself. I needed people in the coalition who would have the courage to speak out, and who would do so knowing full well that there would be consequences for doing so. As Shirley Marsh of Yes Biscuit once wrote:

> "In reality, [animal shelter reform] takes a group of dedicated animal advocates willing to stir things up in their own community by challenging the status quo and refusing to accept killing as a means of population control. There are consequences to such actions: old

friendships may be broken, egos may be bruised, glass houses may be shattered. This ain't no fairy tale. It's hard work, which will be met with resistance by some. You will no longer be able to ride the I Love Everybody and Everybody Loves Me bus. You will not be nominated for homecoming queen. No soup for you.

Like all things in life, working to end the killing in your community is a choice you must make for yourself. You can choose to carry on with the 'save a few and kill the rest' status quo. You'll get to keep all your Facebook friends and play Farmville with them in between posting pets from kill lists. Or you can choose to reject the idea of needless killing as justifiable in any way. You'll make some people feel uncomfortable, and they will resent you for it. But you'll have the opportunity to educate and learn from others who are on the same path. No longer will you feel an awkward compulsion to defend those who kill friendly pets in shelters while simultaneously advocating to save shelter pets. You will have the clarity of mind that comes from knowing where you stand."

The mission of No Kill Huntsville was, and has remained, to encourage the City of Huntsville to stop the outdated practice of destroying healthy and treatable pets using tax dollars. Existing no kill communities across the country do not have anything Huntsville does not have, so there was no reason we could not follow the same path as those places and keep animals alive.

Because Huntsville is also called the "Rocket City," the mind-set was simple: Saving pets is not rocket science, and even if it were, that's okay. We have people for that.[15]

I fully intended to promote the No Kill Equation with the group from the start. It worked in other areas of the country, and there were lots of people we could connect with for the research phase of our organization and for future networking purposes. We didn't have to re-invent the wheel. We just had to figure out what other people were doing and try to bring those progressive ideas to Huntsville.

In addition to promoting the No Kill Equation as a sheltering philosophy, I felt strongly that we should focus not on the shelter director herself, but instead on the concept of municipal accountability and municipal leadership. Multiple city officials were responsible for the operation of Huntsville Animal Services and focusing on one person who had limited authority would not bring about the long-term change we sought.

This is the vision I drafted to post on our website:

Picture this:

A press conference is called by the City of Huntsville. The public is invited to attend. Media outlets are there. At a podium stand the

---

[15]One of the original members of No Kill Huntsville is, in fact, a rocket scientist. She works for NASA, does projects in support of the International Space Station and leads a local rescue group that helps free-roaming community cats and removes cats from the animal shelter.

mayor, city administrator, and shelter director. They are accompanied by a host of local public officials, public figures, animal rescuers, and animal advocates, some of whom have leashed dogs with them. And the press conference begins.

The mayor announces that a decision has been made to make Huntsville and the Madison County region a no kill community. He tells all those present that after some soul searching and networking with people across the country, the city has decided it is no longer going to destroy healthy and treatable animals using our tax dollars, because doing so is just not consistent with our culture, with the values in our community, and with the values in our country. He says that there is much work to be done. That making this transition will take the support of the entire community, but that he and city leaders have decided to draw a line in the sand and take a leap of faith that we can, and must, do this for the sake of the people who live and work here, and for the sake of the animals we say we love. We are already known as a great place to live and work, and we have an impressive resume as a community, but we want to add the description no kill community to our list of attributes.

The mayor goes on to say that he is convinced we can do this because so many other communities have taken this step before us. We are the Star of Alabama. The Heart of the

Tennessee Valley. We are smart, progressive, and creative. And we will lead the way for our state and show that we can save the lives of animals that are homeless or lost while saving tax dollars in the process.

This is our vision. This is our goal.

The members of No Kill Huntsville banded together to speak with one voice for the sake of our community. We support and promote the No Kill Equation because it has been proven to work in every community where it has been fully implemented. It balances public safety with animal welfare and fiscal responsibility. It's just a smarter way to use our existing resources, it does not take increased cost output, and saving the lives of animals stimulates our local economy.

It is a decision. It is a choice. Please join us as we seek to make this vision our reality.

I had a plan and just hoped that others would agree to help. It was time to put actions behind our beliefs and start rocking the community boat to achieve change.

The Research

The first meeting of No Kill Huntsville was held on January 23, 2012, almost three years to the day after I first met with the mayor, city administrator, and shelter director. The live release rate for 2011 had been 34 percent; two out of every three animals had been destroyed.

About two dozen people came to hear my pitch about the coalition and how we would go about encouraging the city to change the way the animal shelter operated using tax dollars. I was looking for people to commit and say, "I'm in" for the long haul.

We met once a month for a period of months. As time went on, the size of the group shrank. Some people were uncomfortable with the concept of political advocacy. They worried about how it would reflect on them personally, worried about how it would reflect on the organizations and businesses with which they were associated, and worried about being part of a group that planned to be outspoken. They worried about whether the plan would work. As much as most people in the original group said they wanted things to change at the animal shelter, they didn't want to be *too* confrontational about it or come across as being too aggressive.

We agreed that there was truly no polite way to say, "Please stop killing healthy and treatable animals," but many of the people who attended the first few meetings were just not ready to take a stand. Others supported the shelter director personally and were not able to separate the result (dead animals) from the person they felt was doing her best to run the shelter with the resources she had. Others left the group because they could not carve out time to be involved on an ongoing basis. A few people were removed from the group when their presence proved disruptive.

We established our No Kill Huntsville website and our Facebook page in April 2012. We planned to use social media as a tool, but our primary platform for sharing our philosophies and vision was, and has always been, the website. Both included a color logo of people holding hands around a dog and cat with the tagline, "saving animals through advocacy."

We ultimately ended up with a group of 11 people who agreed to participate and speak with one voice. We agreed to promote the No Kill Equation as the solution to help the shelter improve and we agreed to share research tasks that would later be used to approach the shelter director and other city officials. Members of the group were tasked with reading *Redemption* to familiarize themselves with the No Kill Equation, which we discussed at length. The elements of the equation were then divided up among group members (some of whom worked as teams) to be evaluated. We had to:

- determine what programs and procedures the shelter was already using related to each element;
- network with no kill contacts in other states to ask what they are doing in their shelters for each element, and;

- develop recommendations we could make to the city on how to implement the programs in Huntsville.

We first did our best to determine what programs and procedures were already in place at the shelter. Some of our members led nonprofit shelters and rescue groups that interacted with the shelter director regularly, and they were able to provide details. We also contacted the county animal control director, who engaged with the city animal shelter daily, to get his input on existing programs and policies.

For networking, we reached out to contacts in seven states: Nevada, Texas, Minnesota, Michigan, Maryland, South Carolina and Virginia. We were able to get some details about the programs and methods they had developed (sometimes through trial and error) and used regularly. It was incredibly helpful to engage with people who had walked this path before us and knew what looked good on paper compared to what worked in a real-world way. They were all happy to help us and agreed to remain our networking contacts moving forward.

To develop recommendations, we compiled our information and created a chart for each element of the No Kill Equation. We pointed out what tasks or steps could be performed by volunteers, and what components could be implemented without increased spending or by using grant money. Examples of our research are shown below.

Pet Retention Programs (keep them out)

What we have/do now:

- animal issues information on the shelter website
- working with a couple of trainers for dogs with behavioral challenges

What other places do/ what we may need:

- pet surrender by appointment to provide pet surrender counseling (with the help of volunteers) to talk about issues that may be overcome so the pet remains in the home, is rehomed by the owner or is fostered short-term
- provide assistance by phone to families with animal issues to decrease the number of pet surrenders to the shelter (using help of volunteers and a help desk book such as that used by Nevada Humane Society)
- provide more comprehensive information on the shelter website to encourage pet retention (following other websites such as that for the Williamson County Regional Animal Shelter and Wonderpuppy.net)
- partner with obedience trainers and animal behaviorists to sponsor classes at the shelter or off-site once a month to overcome issues (separate classes for dog owners and cat owners)
- offer a free training session for anyone who adopts a dog through the partnership with obedience trainers and animal behaviorists
-

Comprehensive Adoption Programs (get them out)

What we have/do now:

- set adoption hours Monday to Friday and Saturday (primarily when adults are at work and children are in school)
- monthly adoption promotions at the shelter
- recent city council approval to do adoption promotions and specials
- some off-site adoptions using volunteers

What other places do/what we may need:

- hold a widely publicized adopt-a-thon to serve as an open house event and a way to get animals adopted fast
- ongoing community outreach/education to dispel the myth that shelter animals are damaged
- ongoing off-site adoptions at various locations around the city/county (dog park, city parks, businesses, stadium)
- modify the weekday adoption hours to facilitate adoptions and customer service (not more hours; different hours)
- be open to the public for adoptions limited hours on weekends and holidays to make it easier for people to adopt
- well-publicized, ongoing adoption programs for special groups in our area for which the adoption fee is waived: pets for patriots, seniors for seniors, hounds for the homebound, cat companions (homebound people)

- monthly adoption specials: name your price, two for one, back in black, promotions tied to holidays or events
- offer free training to anyone who adopts a dog (by partnering with trainers/behaviorists for a class once a month)
- make adoptable animals visible in the community with volunteers (in parks, near stores, at events)

We completed the research in early 2013. Our goal was to seek a meeting with the shelter director and city administrator. He hoped to present our vision for Huntsville as a no kill community, and to talk through the elements of the equation in hopes of developing some plan to work with city officials toward implementing the programs of the No Kill Equation (and while encouraging them to network with the same contacts we used for our research). That was our ask.

The First Ask

As 2013 began, the live release rate for the prior year was 41 percent. It had gone up slightly from the prior year, but progress was incredibly slow. More than half the animals entering the shelter in 2012 had been destroyed.

We met in January and February to confirm our plans for a meeting with city officials. We agreed that one person would speak for the group to start, and then the people who had done the research for each element would speak to that element while providing copies of our research. We hoped to schedule a meeting in March.

Our intent all along was to make the ask as politely as possible. If the city agreed to consider no kill philosophies using our research and by networking with our contacts, then the need for political advocacy would be diminished and we could have offered support and volunteered. If the city did not agree to consider changing the culture at the shelter, then we would have no alternative but to seek the support of the community.

As we were making final plans to seek a meeting with city officials, we learned that a subject matter expert from Minnesota, Mike Fry, planned to be in the state to speak with city officials in Scottsboro, Alabama. We knew of Fry from our research and his decades of work at The Animal Ark in Hasting, Minnesota.[16] He had

---

[16]Mike Fry's mother, Marleen Foote, is arguably one of the first no kill advocates in the United States. She founded The Animal Ark in 1977 and was promoting no kill philosophies at a time when approximately 17 million shelter animals were

decades of experience in animal sheltering, is considered a leader in the no kill movement and is considered an incredible resource for advocates hoping to change their own communities. An advocate in Scottsboro (who was part of No Kill Huntsville for a short period of time) arranged for Fry and another no kill advocate named Kelly Jedlicki, from Kentucky, to visit and speak with city officials about no kill programs. We learned that they planned to give a presentation at Huntsville Animal Services while they were in the area. We honestly tried to keep that from happening; we were incredibly close to seeking our meeting to do the ask, and we did not want that process taken off course. By the time we learned of Fry's visit, plans had already been made for him to speak, so we paused our efforts to see what came of his Huntsville visit.

We were not present at the animal shelter on March 26, 2013, when Fry and Jedlicki gave a presentation to city officials at the shelter. Fry told us later that the shelter director said during his visit that our area lacked talent and that she was making a lot of progress despite many challenges. He also informed us that he had offered to return to Huntsville to provide confidential consulting services after having been told he would understand the situation better if he spent some time in Huntsville.

Over the course of the next month, Fry made multiple attempts to contact the shelter director to plan a return

---

being destroyed annually across the country. Fry once described his mother's no kill advocacy in the 1970s this way: "It must have been like she was screaming inside an empty room."

visit. We were in regular communication with him about our research and our plans to do the ask, so he kept us informed of his progress. Our hope was to have him set a date to return and help the shelter director and her staff at our expense (and at no expense to the city). This was intended to be a confidential visit behind closed doors: no media, no public announcement, just one shelter director with decades of experience helping another shelter director for free and with the single goal of saving animals' lives.

Fry finally spoke with the shelter director on April 29, 2013. He offered to return to Huntsville to help her at no expense to the city and asked for a date when he could return, presuming the offer would be accepted. The shelter director told Fry that she did not want to kill animals, that they were doing a beautiful job and that they were making huge progress. The offer of free consulting help was declined. [17]

When Fry's efforts to return to Huntsville to provide free consulting services were rebuffed, we felt as though our ask had been answered, and the answer was a resounding no.

---

[17]Fry told us that the free help was declined because the shelter director could not hear the message from him. We never understood this. It seemed illogical to decline an offer of free help from an expert, particularly when lives were at risk.

The Workshop and Another Ask

After the shelter director's interaction with Fry, we decided as a group to forgo a direct meeting with city officials for the time being. Fry was someone with decades of shelter experience who was considered a leader in the national no kill movement. If his help was not accepted, there seemed to be little motivation for city officials to listen to our group.

We had hit the wall again, so we decided to go around it by gaining community support. We knew there was a disconnect—that chasm—between the shelter operation and the public being served. We felt strongly that if we told people what was happening at the shelter and how they could be part of making the culture change, they would support our vision and be encouraged to speak out with us for better use of their tax dollars.

We had already pooled our personal funds together to bring Fry and Jedlicki back to Huntsville and decided to proceed with that plan, but to have them address the public instead. A free public workshop was scheduled for late July, and everyone in the community was invited, including city officials, county officials, elected officials from other areas, rescuers and members of the public. We were told the shelter director and her staff would attend, and we hoped that was the case. It would present an opportunity to bridge the gap between the shelter and members of the public who may never have set foot in the shelter building itself.

We also learned from social media that some shelter volunteers planned to attend the workshop for the sole purpose of being disruptive and making a scene. We could not afford to damage our reputation by being kicked out of the library, so we decided to hire an off-duty police officer to keep the peace. We hosted an online petition about Huntsville becoming a no kill community in advance of the workshop and supplemented the electronic signatures with signatures obtained from the public in person.

Our free public workshop was held July 29, 2013, at the downtown branch of the Huntsville/Madison County Public Library. The conference room was standing room only, and the energy level was high. People were engaged by the presentation about the No Kill Equation and seemed empowered by the information.

The Madison County animal control director attended, as did officials from neighboring counties, but the shelter director and her staff did not. We saw this as a lost opportunity to engage with the public in a positive way. Our fears about disruption by shelter volunteers were quelled by the presence of an off-duty police officer. He asked us, "Why would anyone object to saving the lives of more animals?" Our answer was, "Exactly."

On July 30, 2013, there was a closed meeting at the mayor's office with some members of our coalition, our speakers, and city and county officials. We gave the mayor our petition, asked him to consider making Huntsville a no kill community, and introduced our speakers from the workshop.

The mayor said the shelter was making great progress, and he felt that local rescue groups should be doing more to remove animals from the shelter. He also felt that the reason the shelter was not doing better was the number of animals found running loose in the county. He believed that 60 percent of the shelter intake in 2012 was from the county.[18] We learned during the meeting that the decision for the shelter director and her staff to forgo the meeting had been made by the mayor.

The day following the closed-door meeting with the mayor, the shelter director contacted a member of our group who leads a local rescue group. She and the shelter director began having separate meetings about how to make changes in the shelter. It seemed that the public response to the workshop and the meeting with the mayor had had some effect.

In October 2013, the shelter received a $50,000 grant from Petco following a songwriting competition won by a local animal lover who had adopted dogs from the animal shelter. We recommended that at least part of this grant be used to implement no kill programs in our community by retaining the services of a recently formed shelter-consulting group created by people who had managed one of the largest no kill communities it the country. The recommendation was not followed.

---

[18]The county animal control director told us the percentage of intake from the county in 2012 was 35 percent. Our position was that this number was irrelevant because the city had voluntarily taken on the county contract.

Not Rocket Science

On October 4, 2013, we had a meeting with the shelter director, and some members of her staff to do the ask again. We asked her to implement the no kill programs being used in other parts of the country, asked her to use at least a small part of the Petco grant to hire a consultant to get some help, and asked her to consider using some of the money to take a trip to one of two progressive animal shelters in Michigan and Texas who had extended an invitation for her to visit (at our request). Our ask remained unanswered.

It seemed the wall still loomed before us; we had to stay on subject and keep up our public outreach to bring more people to the issue.

Public Outreach

Our outreach campaign with the public began in earnest shortly after the workshop and continues to this day. We knew we had to keep the term "no kill" on the public radar and take advantage of the workshop's media coverage to generate more public interest.

We ramped up our website content to help people understand the No Kill Equation, myths about no kill philosophies, and what the public could to do help.

We began using social media almost daily to keep our followers engaged and continue their education on no kill programs and what was taking place in no kill communities in other parts of the country. This became a seven-day-a-week effort that continued over a period of years.

We ordered vehicle magnets with our logo and distributed them to reach more people as our supporters drove from place to place. We ordered rack cards that we distributed to local businesses and at local animal-oriented events to help people understand our group and our goals.

We bought space on electronic billboards in different parts of the city and put the term "no kill" on the public radar using positive and empowering content. This was one of our most effective methods of reaching the public because we were able to run multiple images on a single electronic billboard over a period of weeks, as opposed to using a static billboard on which the image does not change (and which is much more expensive).

We chose not to focus on the fact that animals were being killed in the shelter and decided to take the high road in the billboard content. We used images of animals with people accompanied by phrases such as, "We're progressive enough to save shelter pets," "We're creative enough to save shelter pets," "Saving shelter pets reflects our values," "Adopt life" and "Foster life." Our most popular billboard design (based on public feedback) was created by one of our supporters. It showed a dog wearing a space suit with a space-themed background with the slogan, "Saving shelter pets isn't rocket science." The billboards were paid for by members of our group and donations from the public.

We created public service announcements that were distributed to local television stations and that were yet another tool to reach the public in new ways.[19]

We also began to work with the media (television, print, and online) on an ongoing basis so we were always in the public eye. The exposure included articles in a local magazine called *Rocket City Pets*, on Al.com (operated by the Alabama Media Group), on local network television, on local radio, in a local newspaper called *The Valley Planet*, and in the *Huntsville Times*. An article called "Trying to Save Them All" appeared on the front page of the *Huntsville Times* on July 6, 2014. On September 30, 2015, a member of our group published a guest column in the *Huntsville Times* that was

---

[19]One such PSA was later used against us in ways we never would have imagined. More on that later.

balanced by a guest column written by the shelter director.

We showed the documentary film *Redemption: The No Kill Revolution in America* at a local high school. We sent invitations to city and county elected officials, elected officials from other cities and counties, people we considered influential in the community, the shelter director and her staff, our media contacts, veterinarians, and rescuers.

We began seeking the shelter statistics from the city using monthly Public Records Act request letters to the city attorney's office. We did this not just to monitor progress at the shelter, but also so we could keep the public informed of what was happening at the shelter using their money. We reported about the shelter statistics on our website and our Facebook page.

We encouraged people to express what they wanted to local officials, providing them with sample wording they could use in letters and emails. It seemed obvious to us by this point that our efforts alone would not be enough to encourage the city to change, and that it would take public pressure to get the attention of city officials.

We also began promoting periodic Chip-A-Thon[20] events to encourage people to have pets microchipped at

---

[20]These are month-long events during which local veterinary offices provide microchipping services for a low flat rate by walk-in or appointment to help reduce intake at the municipal animal shelter (because the animals can be identified and reunited with owners).

a reduced cost, and we did periodic fundraisers to help the animal shelter.

We blogged on our website regularly about issues requiring more attention than a short Facebook post, such as problems with dogs being destroyed for behavior, transparency in record keeping, and meetings with city officials.

New Leadership

The mayor appointed a new city administrator in January 2014. The city administrator oversees numerous departments and is essentially the first-line supervisor of the shelter director (even though she serves at the pleasure of the mayor). The new administrator is a retired U.S. Army colonel who had served as the garrison commander at Redstone Arsenal. We were hopeful that his military background would bring new oversight to the animal shelter operation. If we could just convince him that saving more animals was what the public demanded and would not cost more money, we may be able to find a way through the wall that had stood in the way of shelter reform for years.

Our first meeting with the new city administrator and shelter director was March 11, 2014. This was essentially the same meeting to do the ask one more time. We shared our research regarding the No Kill Equation and asked the city to commit to ending the outdated practice of destroying healthy and treatable animals in the shelter. The city administrator's answer our ask was a line from the film *Jerry McGuire*: "You had me at hello."

This began a series of meetings with city officials over the course of years, in addition to regular communication by letter on a variety of topics. We repeatedly encouraged the city administrator and shelter director to network with our contacts in other states and consider hiring a shelter consultant who could provide real-world help using proven programs.

In June 2014, the city administrator held a meeting in which he presented a plan for the shelter using a diagram of the No Kill Equation. His diagram resembled a building with a foundation and columns. It was clear that he had been paying attention, had devoted an immense amount of time and thought to the shelter operation, and would help guide the shelter to a new culture in which the focus was on saving lives and not ending them.

By the end of 2014, the live release rate at the shelter had risen to 73 percent—almost double what it had been in the prior year. By the end of 2015, the live release rate had risen to 90 percent.

As time went on, we wrote multiple letters to address our concerns regarding issues such as the community cat diversion program (in which we feared kittens were being released outside), the destruction of large numbers of dogs for behavior, enactment of a Companion Animal Protection Act, and development of a Shelter Disaster Plan (in the event of a mass-intake event). We had periodic meetings with the city administrator to praise the progress being made at the shelter and to discuss our concerns and suggestions for program development.

We made a conscious effort to remain in contact with city officials regularly, to make sure they knew we were paying attention and were still focused on our goals. We took great pains in our communications to be respectful and diplomatic; we often argued among ourselves regarding word choice, to strike a balance between advocacy and diplomacy. We stayed on subject in our support of the No Kill Equation and did not hesitate to express concerns, while looking for opportunities to be complimentary and give praise when it was warranted.

It is not possible for us to quantify the value of our public outreach and the voices of the public communicating with city officials. We know our workshop was standing room only and we know that thousands of people from the city and county signed the petition we presented to the mayor. We also know many people sent letters and e-mail messages to city officials, expressing support for Huntsville becoming a no kill community.

Over the course of five years, the city engaged with three shelter consulting groups to refine programs. One was a consulting group we recommended and for which we split the costs with the city. Another was a group that offered its services for free and arrived after the city had begun making changes.[21] One consultant has traveled to Huntsville twice to help train the shelter staff on evaluating dogs and using programs to keep dogs from degrading (our group members covered a portion of the costs).

Although the city did use consultants, we knew that the presence of fresh leadership in the city was making a huge difference, not only in the shelter, but also in our

---

[21]This organization (which no longer exists) focused on a 90% live release rate as the goal (with which we choose to differ). It went on to market its services to other cities using Huntsville as an example. The consultants helped the shelter director in ways we could not because she was open to their approach and listened to what they had to say. Much of their funding came from a famous actor.

relationship with city officials. We were finally able to have conversations with someone who would listen to what we had to say, who told us about the city's plans, and who did not take our comments personally.

We also felt (and still feel) that but for our advocacy, little would have changed regarding the shelter operation. Progress was being made, but it was incredibly slow. Having new leadership who not only felt strongly about saving the lives of animals but who also understood the time sensitivity of changing the shelter operation—and heard us—was a giant step forward. The new city administrator was on board from the start. From what we could deduce, he gave the shelter director the direct support she needed which helped give her the courage to change the culture in her department.

Regarding the speed of progress, the shelter director herself told an audience at a national animal welfare conference in late 2017 that she spent too many years moving slowly to save lives when she should have been acting with a greater sense of urgency. She compared her progress to the fable of the tortoise and the hare, calling herself the tortoise and encouraging others to be the hare and not to delay in embracing change.

Our most recent meeting with the city administrator as of this writing was held in August of 2021. He repeated a position he had stated in many prior meetings: that the City of Huntsville has not destroyed any healthy and treatable animals since October 2014.

The live release rate at Huntsville Animal Services has exceeded 90 percent for both dogs and cats since 2015.

At the time of first printing of this book, the 2018 live release rate for dogs was 90% and the live release rate for cats was 96 percent. The live release rate in 2020 was 93% for dogs and 96% for cats.

The Opposition

For all the good things that happened once new leadership was involved, the process was an incredible struggle in many ways.[22]

When we formed No Kill Huntsville, we anticipated that there would be opposition to our efforts. We expected resistance from the shelter director and her staff, from shelter volunteers, and from some members of the community. We also expected a degree of opposition from the rescue community, as illogical as that may seem.

The initial opposition came from people who considered themselves animal advocates, people who were present at our early meetings of No Kill Huntsville. Although most of the people invited to become part of our group said they wanted the shelter to stop destroying healthy and treatable animals, many were not able to separate the result (dead animals) from the shelter director, who they felt was doing her best to run the shelter with the resources she had. Some were certain she was doing all she could. Others felt that advocacy was too direct and were uncomfortable with the fact that we planned to

---

[22]We explain this information in detail because opposition often causes animal advocates to walk away from advocacy, or to spend too much time trying to persuade staunch opponents with whom there is no conversation to be had. Knowing how the opposition thinks and behaves can be almost as important as knowing why the No Kill Equation works.

publicly call out the killing while encouraging the city to change how the shelter operated.

One member invited to the group based on a recommendation from an existing member was openly disruptive, arguing about the shelter statistics we had calculated. When more than half of the animals entering the shelter are destroyed, it was of little importance whether our statistics were only a few percentage points apart from this member's statistics. It was enough that animals impounded in the shelter had less than a fifty percent chance to get out alive.

The second source of opposition was from the shelter director. When she professed in the April 2013 telephone call that her shelter was doing a beautiful job, she no doubt genuinely believed that; progress was, in fact, being made. Our position was that it was just incredibly and unnecessarily slow and that with each day of delay, the lives of more animals were ended when they could have been saved.[23]

There are examples of shelter directors who have learned that there are better ways to function to keep animals alive and have adjusted their methods accordingly. The Upper Peninsula Animal Welfare Shelter in Marquette, Michigan, is one such example (among many); the shelter leadership read *Redemption*, evaluated how the shelter was managed and decided to embrace the No Kill Equation to save lives.

---

[23]Between 2008 and the end of 2013, more than 33,000 animals were destroyed at the animal shelter.

The reality is that many shelter directors are resistant to change. The fear of failure can be so paralyzing that it is easier to defend—fiercely—the status quo. They fear that if they make it known that they plan to save more lives and then fail, that may expose them to criticism. There has never been a community of which we are aware where trying to save the lives of more animals has led to destroying more animals. Any progress is progress.

Many shelter directors also resist change out of fear they will open themselves up to blame. If a shelter director educates himself or herself and begins saving the lives of many more animals, he or she may be criticized for the hundreds or thousands of animals previously destroyed. While this is possible, it seldom happens. When shelters change their culture and more lives are being saved, people do not focus solely on the past; they focus on the future and the lives of the animals who will be saved moving forward.

We tried to get our shelter director free help, and she declined. This decision put our group on a different path than we had hoped to pursue. If she had agreed to free help, it could have forged the beginning of a cooperative relationship in which we could have helped her network with her peers or helped her develop programs that could have been implemented over time. The denial of free help caused the shelter reform process to take longer than it otherwise would have taken.

The most vocal and toxic opposition came later, from an unlikely source: people in the rescue community. From the time we set up our Facebook page, we were subjected to incredibly hostile and inflammatory comments from people who did not agree with our goals. Although we tried to use the page to educate people about no kill philosophies, such education was often impossible. We ultimately banned dozens of people from our Facebook page because there was no conversation to be had.

We viewed our page as akin to a lecture hall at a university. No professor would allow a group of unruly students to storm a lecture hall, take control of the podium and espouse their own version of reality. Our page, our message. We did our best to be respectful to people and encourage them to spend their time in better ways than bashing us on Facebook. People who continued to be hostile or disruptive were banned from our page; there was no point in trying to convince people who did not believe in our vision at all.

In October 2015, we published an image on Facebook that we called a no kill report card, on which we gave the animal shelter a grade for each element of the No Kill Equation. The grades ranged from a B for Community Cat TNR programs to an F for Pet Retention Programs. Each grade was explained.

The reaction to the report card was swift and hostile. Within a week, a hate page was created on Facebook directly related to our group. The page used a modified version of our logo with similar colors and figures. While our logo used the tagline, "saving animals through advocacy," the hate page logo was, "working together to achieve nothing."

Most of the posts on the hate page were re-posts of our content on the No Kill Huntsville Facebook page. The hate page shared our posts and prefaced them with snarky and hostile comments. Some original content posted on the hate page tried to discredit the nonprofit organizations managed by some of our members, as a way of finding fault with individuals and directing attention away from the subject of our advocacy.

Perhaps the most shocking post on the hate page was a short video. Someone took the time to extract the sound from a public service announcement we had provided to local television stations to promote our vision (and was also uploaded to Youtube). The extracted sound file was combined with a video so that it made it appear as if my voice was coming from a monkey's rectum.

We were not sure at the time who established the hate page, but the supporters became obvious from "likes" and comments to the content. The supporters included shelter volunteers, rescue group volunteers and fosters, the vice president of one local rescue group, and the shelter director herself.

We monitored the page for months. We did not comment or do anything to add fuel to the fire. After the shelter director had liked multiple posts, a member of our group filed a formal complaint with the city administrator about the shelter director for conduct unbecoming a city official. Her comments were removed, but the page remained. A couple of months later, we concluded that a shelter employee had established the page, and we implored the city administrator to take steps to have the page deleted. The page was deleted in February 2016.

One tactic that opponents use to try to redirect the conversation is to complain that no kill advocates should be more diplomatic and show more respect in communications. Opponents attempt to focus on the messenger, to divert attention from the message being necessary in the first place. Even when advocates take the high road, as we took great pains to do, opponents make inflammatory statements to the effect that the advocacy is nothing more than personal attacks.

We of No Kill Huntsville never engaged in personal attacks. And we most certainly never resorted to the sort of juvenile behavior shown over a period of months on the hate page. We were left to wonder how much could have been accomplished by those same people had they only focused on the philosophies and programs we were working so hard to promote.

We learned through experience what other no kill advocates before us knew: Diplomacy is not always a two-way street, and there is not always a conversation to be had with people who either stand in the way of animal shelter reform or who disregard advocates as being uninformed and naive.

Now that the shelter has made tremendous progress, our critics have gone silent, for the most part. There is little they can say to fault us; our methods have proved true.

We learned what other no kill communities before us learned: saving lives is about the culture in the animal shelter because that is the place where animals have historically been killed. Although the behavior of the public being served relates directly to the ability of any animal shelter to provide quality services, the fact that animals die in shelters cannot be blamed solely on the public. The public in Huntsville and Madison County, Alabama did not suddenly become more responsible; the public was interested in saving the lives of animals all along. What changed to save more lives was the shelter operation itself.

We also have an improved relationship with the shelter director now that tremendous progress had been made. We criticize less and compliment more, looking to give credit where it is due. We work hard to keep the animal shelter in the public spotlight using media sources and by keeping our followers engaged on our website.

Most of our individual members have positive relationships with the shelter director for the sake of the greater good, and we communicate with her regularly. One of our members has done fundraisers for the shelter and recently worked with the director to advance an ordinance that requires pet shops inside the city limits to source dogs and cats for sale from the animal shelter and local rescue groups (and does not allow importing animals from breeders or brokers for sale).

We know that a lot of animals died during the years when progress was slow. We choose to not focus on that fact and instead focus on the fact that city officials have worked so very hard to change the animal shelter from a place of death to a place of new beginnings for the animals entrusted to their care.

The Huntsville Animal Protection Act

We began promoting the concept of a Companion Animal Protection Act (CAPA) for Huntsville with our followers, the city administrator, and members of the city council in 2016. The shelter had made tremendous progress; no one wanted to go back to the old ways of functioning when so many animals died. We felt the next logical step was for the city to enact a CAPA ordinance. This is local legislation that sets basic standards for the operation of the animal shelter, codifying the standards so they are maintained regardless of who runs the shelter and who leads the city.

Our first attempts to promote a CAPA did not get far. The city administrator seemed generally interested in the idea but was not interested in codifying any standards regarding the shelter.

In April 2017, the mayor announced his plans to run for governor of Alabama. He is well respected in Huntsville, and we felt he had a real chance at being elected. In early 2018, we began meeting with members of the city council to promote a CAPA more directly. We called it the Huntsville Animal Protection Act. Some of the provisions were:

- irremediably suffering animals would be euthanized without delay, upon a verbal or written determination made by a licensed veterinarian;
- the shelter would take action to ensure that all animals are checked for all currently acceptable

methods of identification, including microchips, identification tags, and licenses;

- stray animals with significant health conditions could be transferred to a private sheltering agency or rescue group immediately after intake, subject to the same rights of redemption by the owner;
- the shelter would provide all animals with environmental enrichment to promote their psychological well-being such as socialization and regular exercise;
- the shelter would develop and follow a care protocol for animals with special needs, such as nursing mothers, un-weaned animals, sick or injured animals, geriatric animals, or animals needing therapeutic exercise;
- the areas in the shelter where animals are housed would be cleaned at least twice a day to ensure environments that are welcoming to the public, hygienic for both the public and animals, and to prevent disease;
- the shelter would not destroy a savable animal unless and until it has made an emergency appeal to all organizations on an established registry that the animal is at risk (with at least forty-eight-hour notice) and without documenting lack of an appropriate foster home placement;
- the shelter would not destroy a savable animal as long as there is open kennel space to house that animal; this includes dogs socialized to humans but who may not get along with all other

dogs (being mindful that dogs will sometimes get along with some, but not all, other dogs);

- the live release rate at the shelter would not dip below 90 percent in any twelve-month period for dogs and cats, and if it did fall below that rate, the shelter director would document the reason for that fact in a written report that attests that no healthy or treatable animals were destroyed and that only those animals who were suffering, irremediably ill or who constituted a genuine public safety threat were destroyed.

Our initial meetings with members of the city council went well. We had two council members who agreed to sponsor the HAPA, and two others seemed interested in supporting it. We referred to the HAPA as legacy legislation intended not to micromanage a city department, but instead to preserve the legacy of city officials moving forward by ensuring that certain standards were met.

The mayor did not win the primary election for governor—a relief for us in some ways. The progress made at the animal shelter had become a point of community pride, and we felt the subject would remain important to him if he remained in local office. We then moved on to meeting with candidates for an upcoming city council election to see if they would support the HAPA. All said they would.

In August 2018, we learned from one of our council sponsors that she had been meeting with the city administrator about the HAPA. We initially thought it would be handled as a single ordinance added to the city code. We learned in September that the city planned to update existing Chapter 5 of the city code, which governs the subject of animals for the entire city. This means that it covers not just the animal shelter operation, but also laws about licensing, animals running at large, violations, and penalties for those violations.

In October 2018, we learned that the HAPA as we had written it would not be included in the city's revisions to Chapter 5 of the city code, but that about 80 percent of what we had proposed would be included. One of the provisions we felt most strongly about—the language about the live release rate not falling below 90 percent—did not make the cut. We were told that the city did not want to legislate outcomes. We were disappointed, but we waited to see the draft of the proposed ordinance before rushing to judgment. [24]

The first reading of the new ordinance was scheduled for a city council meeting on October 25, 2018. We thought we would see the ordinance draft prior to the council meeting so that we could make comments during the meeting. We did not. We attended the meeting and listened to the shelter director's presentation to the council about the changes to Chapter 5. She said running the shelter was a labor of love and her life's passion. It was refreshing to hear the shelter director speak so passionately about her job and about her plans to

---

[24] A live release rate is not a goal; it is an indicator of an animal shelter that has implemented at least some progressive programs. We sought this provision in the HAPA as a stopgap measure to prevent the shelter operation from reverting to prior operating methods.

remain committed to saving lives while providing excellent public service.

Following the presentation, one of our city council sponsors said the following to the shelter director and the members of the audience attending the council meeting:

> All of us had visits from our friends at No Kill Huntsville, and they're here with us this evening. I want to acknowledge them and their efforts. Timing is everything. They came to us with some concerns and some suggestions in the form of a Huntsville Animal Protection Act. The timing was great because [the city administrator and the shelter director] were in the process of going through this ordinance, and so they were able to take that input and incorporate it in this ordinance. I know there was a lot of discussion, and I know No Kill Huntsville wanted that 90 percent number in there, but instead what we have are two "whereas" [clauses]. One is celebrational and one is aspirational.

> The first one is, "whereas the City of Huntsville has increased opportunities for the live release of its shelter animals while balancing public safety and animal health and welfare." That's the celebration of the work that you have done, and you need credit for that. And then all the partners, because I know you couldn't have done it without a lot of the folks who are

working with you to make that possible, so that's a thank you to them as well.

The second is aspirational, "whereas the City of Huntsville shall remain dedicated and steadfast toward all of its existing life-saving programs and, as needed, the creation and development of additional life-saving programs." That's where this city can do better than 90 percent; 90 percent becomes that floor otherwise, and we can do better. This is a commitment to doing more than 90 percent. It's in our policy here. I also appreciate the fact that you have gone beyond that and broadened the scope of this ordinance and included some things that you've been doing and those that you hope to do and you hope as a community we can do. This is a very broad way to address all of our challenges to keep our pets safe, keep our community safe, and make it a better place for all of us.

We obtained a copy of the draft ordinance to amend Chapter 5 of the city code the following day and provided our input to the city for minor revisions. The Huntsville City Council voted unanimously in favor of the new ordinance (which included some of our requested changes) on November 1, 2018.

We did not get the HAPA in quite the form we had hoped. What we did get was strong language about the city's plans moving forward, strong language regarding the shelter operation, and assurances that some of the language included in the HAPA would be included in policy revisions rather than being codified as part of the law for the city.

The ordinance contains the following statements of intent and provisions for operation of the animal shelter:

Not Rocket Science

Statements of Intent

WHEREAS, the City of Huntsville values the life of each and every one of its shelter animals, and therefore strives to provide these animals with the Five Freedoms of Animal Welfare, which are freedom from hunger and thirst; freedom from discomfort; freedom from pain, injury, or disease; freedom from fear and distress; and freedom to express normal behavior; and

WHEREAS, the City of Huntsville recognizes and accepts the substantial responsibilities that come with proper sheltering and caring for its shelter animals; and

WHEREAS, the City of Huntsville will provide proactive field services by prioritizing education and the provision of resources and information, discretionary of the issuance of code violations or citations; and

WHEREAS, the City of Huntsville has increased opportunities for the live release of its shelter animals, while balancing public safety, and animal health and welfare; and

WHEREAS, the City of Huntsville shall remain dedicated to and steadfast toward all of its existing life-saving programs and, as needed, the creation and development of additional life-saving programs; and

WHEREAS, the City of Huntsville is firmly committed to an adoption and placement decision process that does not discriminate against or disparately impact any minority or underserved populations, while striving for efficient customer service; and

WHEREAS, the City of Huntsville recognizes the vital role that robust volunteer programs are to its life-saving programs, and that the maintenance and development of these programs provide improved opportunities for both its sheltered pets and the visiting general public; and

WHEREAS, the City of Huntsville seeks to quickly and reliably return pets to their owners; and

WHEREAS, the City of Huntsville attempts to identify adoption or placement options for the shelter animals in care, while recognizing discretion is necessary to make the best decisions for animals and the communities in which they live; and

WHEREAS, the City of Huntsville shall continue to provide operational transparency by closely monitoring and publishing statistical data; and

WHEREAS, the City of Huntsville seeks to minimize euthanasia through procedural safeguards with a goal of eliminating euthanasia of healthy, treatable animals.

Huntsville Animal Services Policies, Programs and Procedures

The policies, programs, procedures, and activities of HAS, as established by the director, shall be in furtherance of advancing the following goals:

(1) Maximize the live release of all healthy and treatable domestic animals received into HAS care;

(2) Development of routine and positive relationships with private animal rescue organizations to pursue joint programs that facilitate the release of HAS animals into the care of the partner agencies as a component of the department's active foster and adoption programs;

(3) Intake procedures of domestic animals that meet modern standards for shelter medicine and seek to identify the owner of owned domestic animals. All methods of identification should be attempted at intake, including use of microchips and similar emerging technologies;

(4) Foster care programs to provide for the temporary care of HAS animals during mandatory hold periods and while awaiting adoption;

(5) Pre-selection of HAS animals for permanent care solutions during mandatory hold periods;

(6) A single web-based source for listing and advertising all domestic animals at HAS to include initial listing as a component of intake processing of all animals and ensure daily updates to the site;

(7) Defined standards of care of all domestic animals housed at HAS that meet the standards for modern shelter medicine;

(8) Accurate record keeping of all animals housed at HAS. Publish interim monthly reports providing outcomes for animals received at HAS; and following audit, publish an annual report (calendar year based) providing aggregated annual statistics for all animals received and their outcomes. Reports shall be published on the City of Huntsville website for free, public access; and

(9) Required director approval before any euthanasia procedure. Authority to perform euthanasia shall be retained by the director. The euthanasia policy shall include all conditions that must be met prior to conducting any euthanasia procedure.

Not Rocket Science

After Words

History is Important.
Please Don't Change It

It has been said that if we do not learn from history, we are bound to repeat it. It has also been said that to learn from history, it must be factually accurate. When we modify the sequence of events that transpired to get from Point A to Point B, we will learn the wrong lessons.

These statements are universally true regardless of the subject. They are particularly important in the animal welfare movement and, more specifically, in the no kill movement.

The reality is that advocating to save the lives of healthy and treatable animals can be incredibly difficult, even if it should not be. The concept seems simple, right? We want to keep healthy and treatable shelter pets alive and do not want our tax dollars or donations used to destroy them. On the surface, this may seem like a universally accepted position. Most Americans think it should be illegal for animal shelters to destroy animals who are not suffering or who are not genuinely dangerous. I have never met a person who said, "I want my money used to kill animals in need instead of keeping them alive."

Putting the concept into practice is something else entirely. Americans have been housing animals in places we call shelters for over 100 years and have been destroying healthy and treatable animals for as long as anyone can remember. Although the number of animals destroyed in our nation's shelters has declined greatly in the past 40 years, we still kill healthy and treatable animals by the millions. This Orwellian practice is not at all in keeping with our cultural values about companion animals, even though many people have come to accept it as some unfortunate reality.

We are told that animals die in shelters because we just have too many of them, a statement which is entirely untrue. We are also told that animals die in shelters because of the "irresponsible public," who treat animals as if they are disposable and who refuse to spay and neuter pets to keep them from reproducing. There are irresponsible people who should never have pets at all, but it is completely illogical to blame the public for the fact that animals die in shelters while at the same time expecting that very same pubic to make better personal choices, adopt animals, and foster animals.

This whole calcified mindset of, "oh well, we just can't save them all" has led to a culture in which the destruction of perfectly healthy and treatable animals is somehow tolerable, and in which shelters are given a free pass for performing some bizarre public service that is unavoidable. When those shelters are operated by municipalities, or on behalf of municipalities, the amount of time and energy expended to defend the killing can be quite mind-boggling.

Huntsville city officials were introduced to no kill philosophies in late 2008. It is terribly unfortunate that exposure to *Redemption* and other no kill leaders and advocates in 2009 (at the conference in Washington, D.C.) did not cause city officials to act with a sense of urgency to implement the programs of the No Kill Equation. Learning about the No Kill Equation has led to proactive change in other places; it could have been the same in Huntsville.

No Kill Huntsville was formed in January 2012. When the shelter director declined free help in April 2013, we had no alternative but to take the subject to the public. We are now in a position where the live release rate at the shelter has been above 90 percent since 2015, and the city states it has not destroyed healthy and treatable animals since October 2014.

There will always be disputes about exactly what led to the progress we now see. Progress was being made when No Kill Huntsville formed in 2012, but it was incredibly slow; the live release rate in 2011 had been 34%.

There were many factors involved in this process. The decision by the city to implement a spay/neuter program in 2008 to help low income families was incredibly important. It took years to see any measurable reduction in animal intake at the shelter, but it happened over time. The intake has gone from a high point of more than 10,000 animals in 2009 to a low point of 5,100 animals in 2018 (even though the human population served by the animal shelter has grown).

Key to change was the arrival of a new city administrator. He told us in early 2014 that he supported change and that he, too, wanted the city to save the lives of all healthy and treatable shelter animals. He got directly involved in oversight of the shelter operation which is what we hoped he would do as a retired Army colonel with decades of leadership experience.

We have heard the shelter director say (and she has written) that recommendations made by consultants of her choosing in 2015 helped her change the way the shelter operated. We fully acknowledge this to be true; they empowered her in ways we could not, if for no other reason than she was willing to listen to them. We had hoped she would agree to help from an expert consultant in 2013, but she did not. The value of interacting with people who empowered her and increased her confidence level cannot be understated.

The path taken to get to this point, and the struggle faced along the way, are not directly relevant to us here in Huntsville now that we have achieved the goal, for the most part. But those facts are entirely relevant to other communities that may look to our progress and wish to replicate it. We do a disservice to those places if we behave as if our progress was achieved by reaching across differences, finding common ground and all working together to seek a newer and better future. Yes, this community has achieved tremendous success, but it took years longer than it would have taken had city officials sought change many years ago, and without the necessity of advocates speaking out and demanding accountability from the city.

There were literally years when we were advocating for reform while fending off opponents seven days a week. Some of the most hostile opposition came from shelter employees, shelter volunteers, and even leadership of otherwise well-respected rescue groups. While we took painstaking efforts to keep our communications diplomatic and respectful, focusing on municipal accountability and not on individual people, those who opposed our mission did not.

Huntsville is getting a lot of attention these days across the country because of the progress made at our municipal animal shelter. People who live and work here are thrilled with the progress, as they well should be. Shelter animals are now safer here than they have ever been in the history of the community. Huntsville is being referred to as an example of what can happen in the South with a shift in focus and using the compassion that exists in an animal-loving community.

For all our applause of the city for the progress that has been made, the reality in our community is that this process has been a struggle. People who have heard that the City of Huntsville voluntarily made sweeping changes upon learning of progressive no kill programs have been told a sanitized history devoid of many facts.

We acknowledge the value of some of the consultants with whom the city engaged, but the city was making sweeping changes long before any of those consultants landed at the local airport—and has continued to make changes long after those consultants have left. One of those consultancy groups (which no longer exists) focused on a 90% live release rate as the goal animal shelters. It created marketing materials using Huntsville as an example of what it can do. We found this advertising deceptive because only part of the story was being told. We think it is possible people were misled into believing they could replicate the progress made here simply by hiring a consulting organization backed by influential people and large donations.

A similar rewriting of history has occurred related to other locations; it is not uncommon in the no kill movement. Perhaps people are uncomfortable thinking about the more unpleasant parts of the real stories that relate to conflict and struggle. Perhaps it is easier to believe there was no conflict and no opposition to animal shelter reform now that so many lives are being saved. That opposition was difficult to defend because there was no real conversation to be had with people who stand in the way, for whatever reason, of efforts to keep more shelter animals alive.

We firmly believe that but for our advocacy, either little would have changed in Huntsville or change would have taken many more years than it did take. We didn't have the advantage of funding from outside sources or a national platform upon which to stand. Although some funding would have helped, we had what we needed most: determination to bring change to an area and a commitment to see the process through, no matter the personal cost.

Make no mistake: This is not about credit. We have always said that we seek to become irrelevant as a coalition not because we are being ignored, but because we are no longer needed to be boat rockers for community change. We sat silently on the sidelines while others have taken credit for the changes that have been made here, and we plan to continue to do just that.

We know what we contributed, and we know that our efforts led to the tipping point that allowed change to happen. This is not at all about people and patting one another on the back, and it is very much about saving lives. But this is also about being honest about our history so that others can learn from it and perhaps avoid some of the conflict we endured. Much of what took place here was unproductive and led to a higher body count.

A time will come in the history of our country when all municipal shelters are no kill shelters and all communities are no kill communities, because that is what the public wants and will demand. We encourage any community looking at the progress in Huntsville, Alabama, to get ahead of this issue and make changes voluntarily. Listen to the advocates and animal lovers who come to you with ideas, enthusiasm, research, and help. They often know much more about the subject than you may imagine; it is likely they are networked with subject matter experts across the country who can guide your community to achieve change not in years, but in weeks or months. Invest your time and focus into doing what is right so that energy is spent not on struggle and conflict, but instead on saving the lives of the animals we say we love and value.

Our Advice for Advocates and Lessons Learned

We believe that while there are differences between communities in terms of size, resources, politics, and geography, saving the lives of animals is more about a culture than it is about an exact methodology or a cookie cutter solution. Once everyone decides that saving the lives of healthy and treatable pets is a priority right now and not years from now, that is really the first step toward change.

We always promoted the No Kill Equation as a methodology because it can be molded and shaped to fit any community. Any city or county that genuinely wants to end the practice of destroying savable animals need only do some introspection on what is happening currently and work on program development using existing funds and resources. In some places, change can happen virtually overnight. In other places, it takes some time, some planning, some coordination, and a lot of effort to make it happen sooner rather than later.

Animal advocates in other parts of our state and other states contact us regularly for our advice on how they can change the culture in their own communities. We hope that reading our story has helped in some way. Advocates are welcome to use any of the content on our website or Facebook page.

We wish the very best to any person or coalition that advocates to save the lives of shelter animals. Sometimes the only thing standing between animals and certain death is a voice of dissent that says loudly and clearly, "No. This is not consistent with our values and our culture."

Here is our advice for other advocates:

Decide what you want. Ideally, you should be able to state your goal in a single sentence. You cannot fix our entire society or even an entire community in one fell swoop or through magic thinking. You cannot address issues related to companion animals, farm animals, and wildlife at the same time. In our case, we wanted Huntsville to stop killing healthy and treatable animals in the tax-funded shelter. We explained our vision on our website.

Do your research. If you don't know what you're talking about, you'll never make any headway because you'll have no credibility. You need to become an expert on your vision so you can speak intelligently about it at any time to any audience. Learn the history of the issue you are working on so you know how our society got to this point. The best resource to educate yourself is Nathan Winograd's book *Redemption: The Myth of Pet Overpopulation and the No Kill Revolution in America.*

Decide what methods you think work best to accomplish the goal, while being prepared to acknowledge that other methods may have value. Network with people who have walked your path and who are considered subject matter experts. You don't need to be the smartest kid in the class if you know the smartest kids in the class. In our case, we promoted the No Kill Equation from the start. We did local research to learn what was already taking place in our animal shelter and in our community. We networked with no kill communities across the country by phone and email to learn what they were doing related to specific no kill programs. The goal was to share our research with the city, which we did.

Find a few like-minded people—but not too many—to stand with you. It is incredibly rare for a single person to be effective in efforts to make things better for animals. With no support when it comes to addressing systemic issues, particularly with local governments, it's just too easy for you to be dismissed as naive or as a zealot. You will likely be able to accomplish more if you find like-minded people who share your vision and are willing to join you to speak with one voice.

Don't make your group larger than it needs to be for the sake of numbers. You run the risk of ending up with people who say they share your values but who truly do not, or who talk but don't do. Those people can be incredibly disruptive and take you way off course, wasting valuable time and energy. In our case, we began with a large group of people who were invited to participate. People either left the group or were removed over time for being disruptive and not sharing the same vision.

At one point in early 2014, four members of our group left to form a new group to work more closely with the shelter director: Huntsville Pets Alive.[25] This separation

---

[25]The name of this group was based on a similar group in Austin, Texas. When Austin was working toward becoming a no kill community, Austin Pets Alive was a group that

was not adversarial; we saw it as two groups traveling in parallel lanes toward the same destination. While HPA would be more hands-on in the shelter and focus on removing animals to rescue groups, No Kill Huntsville would remain the advocacy group that promoted the No Kill Equation from outside the shelter and continued to seek accountability. The members of HPA continued to meet with the shelter director over a period of months before the organization ceased to exist in any visible way.

We currently have six core members of our group, and we do speak with one voice.

Try doing the ask at the very beginning. If you are trying to reform the way your local animal shelter functions, diplomacy and respect are key, and you simply must take the high road even if that behavior is not reciprocated. We have heard many times that all advocates are abrasive and are too quick to engage in name calling and assigning blame. We are not that way at all. It's not productive. If you do not approach those who have the power to change the situation and simply ask them to consider doing so, you run the risk of offending them unnecessarily. Go straight to the source as your first step. In our case, I paid for the shelter director to attend a No Kill Conference in 2009 in hopes that she would proactively develop programs to save lives. After our coalition formed, we arranged for the director to receive free and confidential help from subject matter experts, with us paying the expenses. The

---

remained apolitical for the most part, while a group called FixAustin engaged in more direct political advocacy.

offer was declined at a time when the live release rate at our shelter was 41 percent. That decision, unfortunately, set the stage moving forward. Had the offer been accepted, much of our advocacy would not have been necessary at all.

Create a platform. We recommend that all advocacy groups have an easily understood name, a simple logo, a fully developed website, and a Facebook page. We recommend use of the term no kill in any group name. This phrase is on the public radar and makes it clear why the group exists: to keep healthy and treatable animals alive. The primary platform to help educate the public should be a website. Facebook is a valuable tool to keep the public informed and engaged; it has some limitations in terms of reaching the public.

Find ways to raise money. All advocacy groups have expenses. We pooled funds for a number of things: website hosting, our domain name, the workshop, our billboards, and expenses for consultants. You can raise money by ordering vehicle magnets that are given away for a donation, or by doing T-shirt fundraisers with a company that pays out the proceeds to a specific organization or individual. There are tax consequences for such fundraisers, and you should consult with an accountant prior to fundraising. We do not recommend that any no kill advocacy group seek nonprofit status and accept donations. The work is inherently political, and there are restrictions on the political behavior of nonprofit organizations, particularly when it comes to promoting certain candidates to the exclusion of others.

Don't waste time or energy on someone who can't hear the message from you. There is no polite way to tell someone, "Animals are being destroyed needlessly. Please stop." But anyone who is really interested in saving the lives of animals, as opposed to defending an outdated process, will quickly let you know that they are interested in learning other ways to function. You cannot force someone to acknowledge your vision and work with you if they are bound and determined not to do so. If you hit a wall, don't keep banging your head against it. Find a way around it by involving the public in your efforts.

That is what happened in Huntsville. We were shocked that the offer of free help was declined. Once it was declined, we took our subject to the public instead. We hosted an online petition that we supplemented with signed petition pages, and we held a free no kill workshop to introduce the public to no kill philosophies and programs. We began a public outreach campaign to bring more people to the subject using the media, billboards, our website, and Facebook.

Make your message one of ethics, money, and accountability—not specific people. All animal shelters function with some oversight. Municipal animal shelters operated by a city, county, or contracted nonprofit are funded by tax dollars. If your argument is that animals are being needlessly destroyed, you will do better to argue that doing so is not consistent with American values, is not a good way to spend money, and that those who oversee the shelter are accountable to the people paying for it: the public. Even if you believe that a shelter director should be removed, you won't get far suggesting that removal unless some actionable form of abuse is taking place. You are better off focusing on those in leadership roles as a whole. If the leadership makes personnel changes, so be it. In our case, we hosted a series of electronic billboards around town for months using empowering slogans such as, "We are progressive enough to be a no kill community" and "Saving shelter pets reflects our values." We kept the public message positive and focused on the fact that our community is capable of saving more lives.

Invite the public to participate in the process. Although most Americans love animals and want the best for them, many people feel powerless to do anything as individuals to bring about change. Studies have shown that the majority of the public believes that the destruction of healthy and treatable animals in animal shelters is unethical and should be illegal. It is important not just to advocate for animals yourself or as part of a coalition, but also to bring the public to the table. A few voices may be heard to a degree or may be dismissed out of hand as naive or uninformed.

When the voting public begins to speak out to officials about what they want done with their tax dollars, the message can be much more effective. Even people who don't share their homes with animals or particularly like animals likely do not want their tax dollars used to destroy animals when those same dollars can be used to save them and bring about systemic change. In our case, we not only took our subject to the public using the media, billboards and periodic events (like our workshop and showing the no kill documentary film at a local high school), but we also encouraged people to speak out as individuals, to tell local officials what they wanted and why. We set up pages on our website to help them find contact information for those officials, and we shared language they could use in letters and emails to help them express themselves in direct and respectful ways.

Don't listen to the haters, enablers, or apologists. Although most people outside of animal welfare circles think that all animal welfare advocates are on the same page, we are not. There are people who advocate for animals solely for the benefit of those animals. They do not seek or want recognition; the act of having helped is their reward. Then there are people who advocate for animals so that they can say they advocate for animals. Many of these people can be your worst critics. For them, advocacy is more about people and not offending anyone than it is about saving lives. Detach from those people and don't let them suck the life force out of you. When you are labeled as the source of the problem because you took it upon yourself to speak out, don't let opponents put the focus on the messenger instead of the fact that the message was necessary in the first place. You cannot win with people who point the finger of blame at you while giving the people destroying animals a free pass.

In our case, we were attacked on social media by rescuers and city employees. We stayed on subject publicly and worked behind the scenes to get the social media attacks to stop, which they did for the most part. We are still told by some shelter volunteers and supporters that our position that all healthy and treatable shelter animals can be saved is naïve and unrealistic. One volunteer said recently that we are "living in a fantasy world." This position does not comport with the city's position that it has not destroyed any healthy and treatable animals for space in years.

Keep the lines of communication open and be respectful. Seeking reform is about advocacy, but it is also about staying on message and about being respectful in communication. Once you begin your advocacy effort, it is important to communicate regularly with those in positions to effect change, and to be specific about what you want or what you are recommending. Part of this process involves the art of diplomacy. While you should be clear and direct about what you want, you must do so with tact and respect to make any headway at all. Look for every opportunity to applaud cooperation or progress. Also keep your communication professional. Email is an overused form of communication, and while it may be convenient for you, it is not always received in the same manner as would be a letter. Seek face-to-face meetings periodically to have open dialogue about what you want while listening to officials about challenges they are facing.

In our case, we communicated with city officials every few months to applaud progress, express concerns, make suggestions, and make it clear that we were not going away. We sent dozens of letters to city officials over a period of three years and we sought and attended numerous meetings with city officials to share our research, discuss program development, talk about progress made, and have an exchange of ideas.

Be prepared to see it through. Once you begin an advocacy effort, the reality is that you can't just stop if you get tired or discouraged. Be prepared to see it through, no matter how long it takes. Your efforts could take weeks, months or even years. Be prepared to stay on subject and stay committed to your beliefs, even if you are not treated with the same diplomacy you use to advocate for animals. In our case, we worked hard to remain in the public eye using the media and social media. We shared our research with city officials during numerous meetings and helped city officials engage with people from whom they were willing to hear the no kill message and who had experience in developing no kill programs. We wrote numerous letters to city officials to offer congratulations on progress and to offer observations about issues we felt still needed to be addressed. We began seeking, and still seek, public records using the Alabama Open Records Act so we can monitor shelter statistics and analyze data regarding the types of animals still being destroyed, and the reason that is happening.

For Rescuers

No Kill Huntsville has support from people in the rescue community, some of whom are part of our group. We also had incredible opposition from people in the rescue community over a period of years. Most of that opposition was incredibly toxic and completely unproductive. While all of us would likely agree that we want the same thing—for animals to make it out of the municipal animal shelter alive—many rescuers worked hard to defend the shelter operation at a time when more than half of the animals were being destroyed. Some did so because they really believed that more animals could not be saved. Others did so because they were so close to the shelter operation (and so convinced the public was at fault) that they could not envision a time when all healthy and treatable shelter animals would be saved. It was just inconceivable to them.

You may know the tale of a boy on a beach, surrounded by starfish that have washed up on the shore. The boy reaches down, picks up a starfish and throws it in the water. A man who sees the boy asks, "Don't you see how many there are? You'll never be able to make a difference." The boy picks up another starfish, throws it into the ocean and says, "I made a difference for that one."

Many in animal rescue circles refer to shelter animals as starfish. As they wash up on the beach, rescuers work individually or collectively to help them. Rescuers often say they cannot save them all, but they can save that one.

163

While it is noble to save those individual starfish, we can do so much more if we take a little time to look at the bigger picture. Where are all these starfish coming from in the first place? Can we keep them from washing up on the shore? Once they are on shore, are there more efficient ways to help them than by trying to do it all ourselves? Can we get the public and the media to help us get them off the beach and on to new lives?

Through the No Kill Equation, we can strive to keep those starfish from washing onto shore. Ways to do that include community cat TNR (trap, neuter, return) programs, high volume/low cost spay/neuter programs, pet retention programs, and proactive redemptions. For those starfish who do end up on shore (meaning in our shelter), we can strive to remove them with the help of volunteers, through foster programs, through comprehensive adoption programs, through medical and behavior programs, and through public relations and community development programs.

The members of No Kill Huntsville hold those who rescue animals in need in the highest possible regard. They are some of the hardest-working people in America and they are to be commended for every life they save. Most rescuers are not compensated for their time and are so busy that they rarely do anything for themselves that others take for granted. Read a book. See a movie. Time is precious, and we all choose how to spend our time. But if we work to look a bit farther out to sea, we find ways to stem the flow of starfish onto the beach. And if we look a bit farther inland, we realize we can involve others in our life-saving efforts. We all know Americans love our animals—our starfish—so we can make this a community effort to save more animals by educating ourselves, educating those around us, and working together.

You may say that you don't have time to read *Redemption*. We say that in order to break the cycle of doing the same thing again and again, you must take time so that you can be part of the bigger picture in which rescuers keep shelter animals alive, but in which rescue groups are not seen as the only solution.

Some have gone so far as to say that rescuers enable poorly performing shelters by doing the heavy lifting and providing little incentive for the shelter operation itself to improve. We don't go quite that far. What we do believe is that many people in the animal rescue community have close relationships with animal shelter leadership and are in the best position to communicate with the people who manage shelters, to gain the cooperation of shelter staff without resistance or defensiveness. Just as the burden of change in any shelter is not that of advocates to carry, it also is not the burden of rescuers to carry. Rescuers can, however, have a great deal of influence on how shelters function if they educate themselves about no kill philosophies and programs, and work from within the system to bring about change.

See you on the beach.

For Shelter Directors and Employees

There have been instances in which shelter directors and staff have learned about no kill philosophies and programs, have evaluated how their shelters operate, and have acted on their own initiative to change the culture. When this happens, as was the case with our contacts in Marquette, Michigan, it is to be applauded.

In our own experience, and the experiences of many of our contacts across the country, change has come not because of steps taken by the shelter leadership or municipal officials, but as the result of public pressure. The public does not want tax money used to kill animals when those same animals can be kept alive using proven programs. When we inform the public about what is happening at their tax-funded shelter with their money (and while they are blamed for it), they get angry and then they get involved. It is then that shelter leadership and officials may listen to the public.

There was an image being shared on social media recently of a veterinary examination room. A dead dog was on a metal table, and a man was sitting on the floor with his head lowered toward his knees. The image made it appear as if the man had killed the dog and was upset.

The caption stated, "You think it's easy to kill companion animals day in and day out." It also stated, "1) adopt from shelters and rescues until they are empty; 2) spay/neuter your pet; 3) volunteer to help if you can." Below the image was the following statement: "Shelters do not want to kill animals, but five million healthy pets die every year. It is an antiquated system that is not good for the workers or the animals. Neutering your pets does make a difference!"[26]

We are not totally unsympathetic to people who go to work in animal shelters with good intentions and then become part of an antiquated system that destroys healthy and treatable animals for space. A lot of people decide to work in the shelter industry because they love animals and want to make a difference.

Our expectations regarding people working in those places is twofold.

First, find out if the shelter destroys healthy animals *before you apply to work there.* If it does, and that fact upsets you, then don't work there. Most people would no sooner work in a kill shelter than they would work in a poultry processing plant or on a hog farm. We all choose where we work, and it's not like "kennel worker" is the only employment opportunity available in your community.

Second, if you are already working at a shelter that destroys healthy and treatable animals, please take the time to educate yourself on how to make that process stop and work to reform the shelter from inside the system. Your silence is truly your consent. No kill philosophies and programs have been common knowledge for about twenty years, and the No Kill

---

[26]The statement about five million animals is incorrect. It is possible this was an image from a few years ago that kept circulating; this is often the case with posts on social media.

Equation has been known for more than ten years. There is really no reason to lament the needless killing of animals because there are ways to stop it.

We are not saying it's easy. Effecting change takes work, planning, and commitment. It takes a change in culture in the shelter to take it from a place where animals are brought to die to a place of hope and new beginnings. If you fear that you will lose your job if you speak out for change, then give some thought to what is most important to you. Perhaps you will find another job that does not cause you to be part of a system that affects your mental health and causes you to lose sleep because you destroyed animals who were not suffering.

We would have responded much more favorably to an image of a shelter worker walking a dog and talking about how enrichment programs are used to keep dogs entertained and to help socialize them.

We would have responded much more favorably to an image of a shelter worker engaged in community outreach to help educate the public to make better choices.

We would have responded much more favorably to an image of a shelter worker engaged in a peaceful protest regarding the continued destruction of healthy and treatable animals using tax dollars or donations.

If the phrase no kill upsets you or if you take issue with shelters being described as kill facilities (as opposed to use of the word "traditional" to describe the shelter), consider what is happening to the lives of animals in the facility. Ending the life of a healthy and treatable animal is a permanent act. It is an act which has consequences and it is not an act of mercy. If someone outside of an animal shelter setting ended the lives of healthy and treatable animals for some reason, we would not call that euthanasia. There is no reason to apply a double standard to what happens outside of an animal shelter to what happens inside animal shelters.

If the death upsets you, don't be complicit in the behavior. Do something to change the system. If you choose to work in a facility that destroys healthy and treatable animals, that is your choice. Just don't expect a whole lot of sympathy from animal welfare advocates. Our sympathy goes toward the animals whose lives were ended unnecessarily. This is an act which is entirely permanent.

We hope the man in the image got up off the floor, quit his job, and became an advocate for shelter reform. We would welcome him to join the no kill movement so we can change our country for the sake of the animals we say we love and value.

We do not expect any shelter to become a no kill facility overnight, although we are aware of occasions when that has happened. We do expect the shelter industry to stop blaming the very public that can help it save lives and to act with a genuine sense of urgency to develop the programs necessary to do exactly that. Just because some people should never have pets does not mean that the public at large cannot be trusted and is completely irresponsible. We believe there is enough compassion in any community to overcome the responsibility of the few, and we have seen that compassion demonstrated time and time again when the public is told exactly how they can help whether it means helping the shelter reduce overcrowding by adopting animals, providing temporary foster homes for animals, providing care for neo-natal animals or volunteering in the shelter to provide enrichment to animals.

We see shelter killing as a disease and no kill programs as the cure. If you are told there is a cure and you refuse to examine it, then you need to find a new job. No kill advocates don't want your job. We want those in the shelter industry to do the jobs they are being paid to do. In the case of those in municipal shelters, you are public servants, and you are paid with our money. It is entirely reasonable and acceptable for us to be critical of how you spend our money when it comes to matters of life and death. We hold other municipal officials to the same standard regardless of their profession: police, fire, public works. If you are not willing to accept any form of criticism from the people who pay your salary, then you need to leave public service and find another form of employment where you are not subject to public criticism.

It is time to lead, follow, or get out of the way.

The lives of animals depend on it.

For the General Public

Animal welfare advocates are not born. They are created through life experiences. Many people come to animal welfare advocacy due to some loss which causes them to dedicate some portion of their lives to a cause. Some come to advocacy due to their upbringing which compels them to speak out for animals as a moral imperative. There are people who learn about the deaths of healthy and treatable animals at their tax-funded shelter who remain convinced there is no other way for the shelter to function. Some go as far as to defend the killing as some Orwellian public service even though it has been proven that there is another way to function to keep animals alive while not compromising public safety.

We encourage everyone to learn what is taking place at their local animal shelter using your money. It may not be enough to just ask. Many shelters which destroy large numbers of animals have stellar reputations with the public because most people do not realize what is taking place behind closed doors. There are shelters which call themselves no kill facilities when they are not.

The easiest way to determine what is taking place using your money is to seek statistics for the shelter and to visit the shelter.

Some shelters make statistics readily available on a website, but you may have to ask the shelter for the statistics. In some cases you will need to submit what amounts to a Freedom of Information Act Request to obtain the statistics from a city official. Provided the statistics included numbers for all animal outcomes (whether alive or not), you will be able to compute the live release rate for your shelter using the information in this book. If the statistics do not include the number of all animal outcomes, you may need to submit a request for that information. If your request for statistics is met with resistance, it is likely you will need to approach a local elected official for help (if the shelter is managed by a municipality) or contact a board member for help (if the shelter is managed by a nonprofit organization which holds the municipal contract).

It is important to visit the shelter to see for yourself how your money is being used. Some shelters are warm, inviting places to visit that are staffed by helpful people who are focused on helping animals while providing excellent public service. Other shelters are dark, depressing places that smell terribly and are staffed by people who do not like their jobs and who behave as if customer service is a burden. Regardless of what you find, remember that you are paying for it.

One of the best ways to evaluate the shelter operation from a taxpayer standpoint are the animals themselves. Few animals behave inside an animal shelter the same way they behave outside the walls of the shelter, but the manner in which they are housed and cared for demonstrates how your money is being used beyond any statisitics you may obtain.
A couple of famous phrases are quoted often by animal welfare advocates.

Lilly Tomlin once wrote the following:

I said, "Somebody should do something about that." Then I realized I am somebody.

Margaret Meade once wrote:

> Never doubt that a small group of thoughtful, committed citizens can change the world; indeed, it's the only thing that ever has.

Please think about those words.

It may seem like a daunting proposition to speak out to seek better for animals. All of us decide what is important to us. We decide which issues in our society we will tolerate and which we will not. Whether you consider yourself an animal lover or you are just interested in tax dollars being spent for the highest and best use, you must decide if animal welfare advocacy is for you. It may very well depend on your level of outrage.

Some people with whom we interact have told us that once they learned what was happening at their local animal shelter, there was no going back. They could not go back in time or just pretend they did not know. It was the knowledge of what happens using their money—and in their name—which caused them to get involved. Steve Shank, who led an advocacy group which pushed Lake County, Florida to reform the animal shelter operation put it this way:

> I didn't know. I feel like I should have known and I wish I knew sooner, but I just didn't. Once I found out what was happening at the animal shelter, I had to do something. There was no

choice to be made. I would not have been able to live with myself, and consider myself a responsible, animal-loving member of my community if I had tried to pretend it was someone else's responsibility to speak out. The responsibility was mine. And now that the lives of animals are being saved, I consider my advocacy to be one of the greatest accomplishments of my life.

I, and the other members of No Kill Huntsville, hope our story has been helpful to members of the general public who may consider speaking out and getting involved. Advocacy is not easy. It takes time, it takes commitment and there is often a price to be paid in terms of friendships lost or opposition from some unlikely sources. In the end, it all comes down to your values and what is important to you.

The tag line on my Paws4Change website is "your values are expressed by the choices you make." The choices you make about what happens at your local tax-funded animal shelter using your money and in your name are entirely up to you.

Our Plan Moving Forward

We did not get the HAPA we had hoped for. What we did get was almost as important. We have local elected officials who are fully engaged and informed about the animal shelter operation. They understand what the word euthanasia means. They understand the phrases "no kill" and "live release rate." They know that they will need to provide more resources moving forward to help keep animals alive. They also know that it is possible to operate an animal services department that keeps the public safe while keeping healthy and treatable shelter animals alive. This is a huge step for any city and is something about which Huntsville can be incredibly proud.

Due to the involvement of city officials and the stated commitment to continue to make progress, No Kill Huntsville has gone dormant for the most part. We always sought to become irrelevant, not because we were being ignored, but because our voices were no longer necessary. If someone had told us in our first meeting on January 23, 2012, that the city could reach a point where more than 90 percent of shelter animals were saved and would enact an ordinance to codify its values, intentions, and expectations, we all would have signed up for that without hesitation.

Even though the live release rate has been above 90% for years, there is still more work to be done regarding animal shelter operations in Huntsville. No one would agree with that reality more than the city administrator and shelter director. Saving the lives of shelter animals is not some goal that is reached, after which things become easier. Saving animals is incredibly hard work every day, and it is work that never ends.

We have some concerns about the focus on 90% as a goal, rather than a benchmark of progress. While saving 90% of the animals is obviously much improved from the past, it should not be the focus. Making it the focus brings with it the possibility that that last 10% of animals will not be provided all available opportunities to make it out of the shelter alive. All animals deserve to be treated as individuals whose lives are of equal value with no regard for statistics.

With advances in shelter operations and veterinary medicine, some shelters are saving as many as 98% of all animals entering the facility; Huntsville is nowhere near that number. We hope for a time when more dogs are saved, particularly medium and large sized dogs who are either overlooked due to perceived breed or who degrade while in the shelter environment and are determined to present public safety risks.

The work yet to be done to fine tune shelter programs will be made easier to a degree now that the city has set a clear path moving forward, and now that the community is personally invested in what happens at the animal shelter using collective resources. People want to help. When the animal shelter explains what help is needed—adopters, fosters, toys, blankets—they tend to rise to the occasion.

No Kill Huntsville's mission is done for the most part because we feel we have reached the limit of our effectiveness at this time. The issues which still exist with the animal shelter operation relate to enrichment for dogs, promotion of dogs, and threatening to kill dogs who show stress in the kennel environment have been present for a period of years. It is up to the city to address these issues proactively. We feel that us repeating ourselves in communications to the city about keeping more dogs alive is of little value.[27]

Our website will remain active for a few years for the benefit of citizens in the community and for advocates in other communities. We will continue to seek shelter statistics and euthanasia reports from the City Attorney's Office each month to ensure the city does not backslide, and to continue our work monitoring the number of dogs destroyed for behavior and kennel stress.

As of this writing, we also plan to promote Chip-A-Thon events annually to encourage people to have their pets microchipped to prevent them from entering the shelter

---

[27]We have long believed that the animal shelter destroys far too many dogs for "behavior" without offering those dogs every possible opportunity to leave the shelter alive. While I was doing final edits on this book, I learned that lesson first-hand. I was at the shelter to record some video footage on a Friday and met a dog named Lulu. She was outside the shelter, being walked by a volunteer. I recorded some video clips of Lulu to create a video project to help market her to the public. I knew she had shown some fear-based behavioral issues inside the shelter. Lulu was happy and walked well on a leash. I touched her. She did not seem the least bit aggressive. Had I met her in any other location, I would have thought she was someone's beloved pet. She was dead three days later, reportedly for behavioral issues.

(or to get them back home quickly) to help reduce shelter intake.

Although we were told by city officials that they did not want to legislate outcomes, we may revisit the issue of the HAPA with city officials at some point in the future so that more elements of the animal shelter operation are codified and can be preserved moving forward no matter who leads the city.

Our Members

The members of No Kill Huntsville became a bonded group over the years. We often disagreed with one another behind closed doors, and there were some philosophical differences of opinion. Looking back, our advocacy was successful because we checked our egos at the door, kept our discussions and plans confidential, and always spoke with one voice to the public and city officials.

The members of No Kill Huntsville are:

Nina Beal, President, The Ark, Inc.
Karen Borden, President, Dixie Dachshund Rescue, Inc.
Dianne Burch, World of Pawsabilities and author of *Maxnificent: The Polka Dot Pyrenees*
Susan Burlingame, Co-Founder, Challenger's House, Inc.
Jane Jattuso, Board President, North Alabama Spay and Neuter Clinic, Inc.
Aubrie Kavanaugh, Manager, Paws4Change.com

Our website is:
www.NoKillHuntsville.com

Our Facebook page is:
www.Facebook.com/NoKillHuntsville

We recommend the following websites to learn more about no kill philosophies and programs:
The No Kill Advocacy Center:
www.nokilladvocacycenter.org

No Kill Learning:
www.nokilllearning.net

No Kill Movement:
www.nokillmovement.org

Acknowledgements

Nathan Winograd has been a long-time supporter of the work of No Kill Huntsville and an invaluable resource. He first published the No Kill Equation in 2007 in his book *Redemption: The Myth of Pet Overpopulation and the No Kill Revolution in America*. A second edition was published in 2009. The book is available on Amazon.com. Kindle versions are often made available for free. The documentary film based on the book is available for viewing on Vimeo. It is called *Redemption: The No Kill Revolution in America*. Winograd's website is www.nathanwinograd.com.

The following people helped us with research and advocacy over a period of years:

Diane Blankenburg, Bonney Brown, Ryan Clinton, Mike Fry, Kelly Jedlicki, Christie Keith, Reva Laituri, Beth Nelson, Mike Martinez, Peter Masloch, Doug Rae, Alan Rosenberg, Cheryl Schneider, Steve Shank, Davyd Smith, Shirley Marsh, Brent Toellner, Bett Sundermeyer, Larry Tucker, and Nathan Winograd.

Thank you to also to Cara Sue Achterberg, Katie Barnett, Kelly Clayton, Leigh Ann Gish, Kim Kavin, Shelley Lomanto, Andy Sieja, Anne Taiz, and Peter Zheutlin for their help.

And the biggest thank you goes to my husband, Rich, who supports me in all that I do.

Not Rocket Science

Author's Note

In August of 2018, I had a meeting with documentary film maker Anne Taiz about the advocacy of No Kill Huntsville related to a film concept she was developing. It was Anne who first recommended I write a book about our path which may help other advocates. I scoffed at the time. Who would read it? Would it really help anyone? I discounted the idea and moved on.

After our work to promote the Huntsville Animal Protection Act was suspended in late 2017, I thought back to how many times we have been contacted by advocates in other parts of the state, other states, and even other countries asking for help. It was then that I decided to write the book, hoping that it would of value to others. Each country, state, and community are different, but some concepts are universal related to the nature of advocacy and the opposition to change.

All the government officials to whom I refer in the book are public officials who are inherently subject to scrutiny and criticism. I have taken great pains to refer to people by title or function and I have purposefully left out parts of the story which I know to be true and which are important to me, but which do not advance the purpose of the book.

I do not consider the Huntsville story to be the success story I had hoped for or which we have seen in other places. It took years for change to occur and there is much work to be done by city officials moving forward, particularly to keep more dogs alive. I still think the story has value if for no other reason than to help people understand some basic concepts and perhaps empower them to speak out for change in their own communities.

Every community has the potential to be a no kill community. Sometimes it just takes the courage to try something new. And sometimes it just takes a group of people willing to band together and speak out with one voice to say, "enough. We are better than this."

About the Author

Aubrie Kavanaugh is an Army veteran who has worked for decades as a litigation paralegal doing defense work; her clients are mostly municipalities and law enforcement officials.

Aubrie became an animal welfare advocate in 2006 after learning about the deaths of animals at her local animal shelter. She manages the Paws4Change educational website, blogs on animal welfare issues, creates video productions and public service announcements for animal shelters and nonprofit organizations across the country, and is involved in advancing animal welfare legislation on the local and state level. She lives in northern Alabama with her husband, their dog, and the enduring inspiration of their dogs to whom they have said farewell for now.

www.Paws4Change.com

Made in the USA
Middletown, DE
30 November 2022

16554144R00113